D0411645

CAMOUFLAGE

Withdrawn From Stock
Dublin City Public Libraries

Leabharlann na Cabraí
Cabra Library
23 DEC 2019

EOIN LARKIN

CAMOUFLAGE

WITH PAT NOLAN

Reach Sport

*This book is dedicated to my wife Anne,
daughters Holly and Ellie and son Mark
for all their understanding and support.
To my mam and dad for their
unconditional love and for the way they
helped me to be the best I could be.
And to friends who have been with me,
in good times and bad.*

Reach Sport

www.reachsport.com

Copyright © Eoin Larkin 2019.

The right of Eoin Larkin to be identified as the owner of this work has been asserted in accordance with the Copyright, Designs and Patents Act, 1988.

All Rights Reserved. No part of this publication may be reproduced, stored in a retrieval system, or transmitted in any form, or by any means, electronic, mechanical, photocopying, recording or otherwise without the prior permission in writing of the copyright holders, nor be otherwise circulated in any form of binding or cover other than in which it is published and without a similar condition being imposed on the subsequent publisher.

Written with Pat Nolan.

Published in Great Britain and Ireland in 2019 by
Reach Sport, a Reach PLC business,
5 St Paul's Square, Liverpool, L3 9SJ.

www.reachsport.com
@Reach_Sport

With thanks to Gill Hess Ltd.

Reach Sport is a part of Reach PLC.
One Canada Square, Canary Wharf, London, E15 5AP.

1

Hardback ISBN: 9781911613459
eBook ISBN: 9781911613497

Photographic acknowledgements:
Tony Woolliscroft (front/back cover images).
Sportsfile, Eoin Larkin personal collection, PA Images.
Every effort has been made to trace copyright.
Any oversight will be rectified in future editions.

Design and typesetting by Reach Sport.

Printed and bound by CPI Group (UK) Ltd,
Croydon, CR0 4YY.

CONTENTS

Eoin Larkin has collaborated on this
book with the Irish Mirror's Gaelic Games
Correspondent Pat Nolan.

Nolan is a best-selling author
and his previous books include
'Life, Death and Hurling – The Michael
Duignan Story' (2011), which was runner-up
in the Irish Sports Book of the Year awards,
and the acclaimed 'The Furlongs – The Story
of a Remarkable Family' (2014).

PROLOGUE

My head hits the pillow and I struggle to sleep with the excitement. In a few short hours the alarm will sound and we'll be bound for the airport for a two-week family holiday, the likes of which we've never undertaken before.

I turn to Anne.

'I can't go to sleep here!'

And then, after another few minutes, I just nod off. When the alarm goes at 1.15am I swat it away, still in that state of wakening confusion, thinking it can't be time for work already, until it all clicks and the tiredness quickly flushes away as I enter holiday mode.

The irony isn't lost on me this night. Three years earlier, to the day, I had stared at the same ceiling, struggling to sleep for vastly different reasons. All sorts of thoughts running through my mind and, yet, nothing running through my mind.

Everything was dull and grim. I didn't know why it was dull and grim. Indeed, I'm not sure I was even acknowledging my mental state at that particular time because if I had known and accepted that this was the case, I would surely have acted on it rather than allowing myself to continually plummet towards oblivion.

This wasn't just a few bleak days here and there. Depression had been swirling around me for a few years but by this stage it had percolated my mind completely. All-Ireland medals and exhilarating days in Croke Park offered no insulation.

In the midst of it all, I was still hurling for Kilkenny but my game had finally crumbled. For years I had managed to play my way around it but I had become a shell of a hurler and, moreover, a shell of a man.

En route to the airport, the kids ask questions that kids ask.

'Are we nearly there?'

'How long are we going to be?'

'How far away are we?'

Questions that I might have growled at three years earlier and thought nothing of. But if that mood takes me now, it challenges me to ask myself *why?* Thankfully, the answers aren't elusive.

As we move through the morning, from the airport to our flight, to another airport and a bus trip before finally landing at our hotel, my thoughts dart back to July 9, 2016, and how bleak my life had become.

And how a single phone call on that fateful morning set my life on a vastly different path.

Brian Cody has long had a habit of doing and saying the right things at the right time. Yet again, he was bang on cue because had that call and the remarkably simple question that followed, the sympathetic ear and the carefully chosen words not been forthcoming, I would have continued to sink further towards a devastating conclusion, with suicide becoming increasingly inevitable.

I'm so grateful that blissful days like this, as we embark on a family holiday, are possible now when they might have been abruptly extinguished.

There's a lot to be said for going to sleep excited at what tomorrow will bring.

1

SEPTEMBER

'Sing it again Daddy, sing it again...'

September is a month that has stirred wildly contrasting emotions in me as my life progressed. In a hurling context, the link is obvious. Only twice in the 12 seasons that I played with Kilkenny did we not reach September. It was the pinnacle that we worked towards. Including replays, I played in 12 All-Ireland finals and won eight, a level of achievement that I couldn't have dreamed of. In my adult life, it's a month that brought me endless joy and glory.

But in my adolescence September was a byword for dread, so much did I absolutely hate school.

#########

I have 11 suits in the wardrobe at home. Ten of them are from All-Ireland finals. We had to make do with the same

13

ones from the drawn finals for the couple of replays that we were involved in! The 11th is the only one that I can tell apart from the others. It's a three-piece and it's grey, whereas the rest of them were two-piece suits and generally dark in colour. The three-piece came as a result of the opening of the Staker Wallace grounds in 2013, when we played Limerick in a challenge game to mark the 30th anniversary of their 1973 All-Ireland win, with JP McManus forking out to have us all suited and booted. It's grand for the lads that worked in the bank, they got the wear out of them, but it's only very occasionally that I slip into any of them. Weddings and that.

You try to make the All-Ireland final as much like any other game as you can but yet you have to acknowledge that it is different. Getting measured for suits is just one part of that. The tailors would arrive at training shortly after we won the semi-final and that would be that, out of the way. It happened so often for us that it just washed over you, but I can see how things like that can be a little distraction for a county that wouldn't be there very often. And you'd be wary of that for new lads on the panel. The older players would have a word to keep them in the loop. 'We'll probably be getting suits now but just go in and get measured then forget about it.'

There's a press night then as well, something we didn't generally do for other games, which some of us would be pulled for. I did a few of them over the years. It never bothered me. As most people will know, we were very good at talking without saying a whole lot.

We'd do the video work on the opposition the week before the final and on the week itself then we'd have a couple of drills to sharpen up on the Tuesday night and a few pucks on the Friday. Then the team would be named and down to Langton's for a bit of grub. I'd find I was always shattered on the day before the final; I don't know if it was nervous energy building up or what. I'd try and have a snooze in the afternoon. I wouldn't go to bed too early that night and would often watch 'Up for the Match' on the television to give me more of a feel for the game. Joe Hayes of Tipperary would always give me a great laugh when he was on. I'd go off to bed then and sleep relatively easily.

Generally we'd meet in the New Park Hotel the morning of matches but for All-Ireland finals it would be Langton's, as that was where we'd end up the following night, win or lose. JJ Kavanagh's bus would ferry us to Croke Park and all our suits would be sent to the Citywest Hotel, waiting for us in the room after the game.

We always went to the Citywest for our post-match banquet and given that there were so many of them doused with liquid refreshment, they almost meld into one. We'd have a couple of pints in Jacob's in Saggart on the Monday before heading to Kilkenny. In the early years we'd get the train and head to the Market Yard to be presented to the crowd; later we'd just get the bus straight down and through the town to Nowlan Park. We'd be well on it by then. Scuttered as we're waving to the masses.

You'd get another couple of days out of it but, without meaning to sound arrogant, we won so often that the celebrations became truncated the longer my career went on and were certainly winding down by Wednesday. You'd go back club training on the Thursday night and you might have a couple in Langton's after it but that was as far as it went.

We didn't reach the final in my first year in 2005 and then it was 2013 before we failed to get there again. It was a little surreal as I watched the draw and replay between Clare and Cork and couldn't really believe what I was seeing. It was extremely open for an All-Ireland final. You score, we'll score and we'll see who comes out on top. There was so much open space and players running straight down the middle. And when you look at it, neither county has got back to a final since, underlining how much of an outlier that year was, even if we could have no complaints with our lot that particular summer.

We didn't tend to get caught up in those sort of games in All-Ireland finals. With us, it was more structured; we impressed the need to close down the opposition and get the hooks and blocks in. We got caught in a free-for-all against Tipperary in 2014 but we amended it for the replay and shut them out.

If I was to give myself a rating for how I played in All-Ireland finals, I would say fair. There were a couple that I played particularly well in but more that I feel I could have made a greater imprint on. I wouldn't put that down to anything in particular and I don't believe it was because they were finals; it's just how things played out.

I felt I did ok for my first final in 2006 though I was taken off early enough. I had a good first half in 2007. 2008 was probably my best final. I felt that I contributed a lot to the 2015 final when Galway had us in a bit of trouble at half-time. I was lucky to have played that day.

Two weeks before the final, on a training weekend in Fota Island, I broke my thumb. On the Saturday afternoon we were playing an internal game and I went to challenge Michael Fennelly in possession. Mick had barely trained that year given his back problems, it was just about managing it as best he could between games. I maintain that if he had been training all year, I wouldn't have broken my thumb because he'd have moved the ball on quicker. The delay allowed me to get my hand in and as he followed through on his swing he nicked my thumb. Straight away, I knew it was broken.

That was confirmed when I went in to Cork with Tadhg Crowley, our team doctor, and had it X-rayed. It was put in a slab and then I went to a specialist when we got back to Kilkenny. He didn't tell me not to play but he put a cast on it to keep it from moving for 10 days. I was to do a bit of running in the meantime to keep myself fit. A couple of days later, I got a call from Brian Cody.

'I just want to know one thing: what way are you going to be fixed?'

'Don't worry about me,' I told him. 'I'll be playing.'

'That's all I wanted to know.'

No matter what was to happen, I was going to play. Richie Power gave me a number for Seán Boylan's herbal clinic and one of his staff, Niamh Guy, sent me down a potion to drink and some poultice to apply. I got the cast off a few days before the final and went up to Dunboyne and met with Seán and Niamh. She stuck some needles in my thumb and manipulated it a little. Straight away there was an improvement: I hadn't been able to use the handbrake in the car on the way up, but I could on the way home.

Tadhg arranged to have a mould put together for me for training on the Friday night but it was digging into my wrist so I reverted to a splint that I had. He gave me an injection before training that evening but my thumb was still quite sore. I met with Niamh again in Mullingar the day before the final and she worked on it a little more. Tadhg gave me another shot right before the game and that one certainly did the trick. I went out and hurled away and never thought about my thumb once. I had one of my better All-Ireland finals, won plenty of ball and clipped a couple of points.

Afterwards, it was badly swollen and I went back into the cast on Tuesday. The doctor in the hospital was foreign. 'You had a broken thumb and then you played a hurling match?' I implored him to cast me up again as quickly as he could to allow me to rejoin the lads in the pub. I was out for about six weeks then which meant I missed the business end of the club championship with James Stephens.

A lot of the other finals I played in were pretty so-so personally. In the early years, there was a tendency for me to be substituted quite regularly. I fell into the trap of becoming accustomed to that and looking to the sideline, waiting for my number to come up. I tried to get out of that by 2007 but it was probably mid-2008 before I felt confident that I would be on the team when going to training on the Friday night before a championship game.

Different finals stand out for different reasons. 2006, being my first All-Ireland, is obviously very special. That day we essentially formed a new template for how we were going to play, some of it unwittingly. We had a very clear structure of what we were going to do – stick to our own men rigidly to ensure that Cork couldn't get their short-passing and running game going. Then, it all went out the window: from the first ball that Seán Óg Ó hAilpín got, we pounced on him. Vincent Hogan, writing in the following day's *Irish Independent*, said that Ó hAilpín was 'promptly set upon like a man who runs out of petrol at the wrong end of town. He was surrounded before the engine began to splutter'. And that set the agenda for the day: we hunted them down relentlessly.

Over the course of my Kilkenny career, we didn't tend to pay much heed to the opposition. I'd say in percentage terms it was usually about 95-5 in terms of us and them.

Brian always instilled in us that if we were right, it didn't matter what the opposition did. But the 2006 final was different. I'd say the balance was tilted to around 70-30. Cork were going for three-in-a-row having introduced a somewhat radical style of play and we broke their game down to a fair degree in the run-up to the game.

We decided to drop deep for their puckout. The full-forward line would effectively regress to where the half-forward line would typically be and the half-forwards would take station at midfield, and so on. We didn't mind if the Cork goalkeeper, Donal Óg Cusack, hit it to a corner-back as we didn't feel that he was going to get significantly greater distance on it than he would. It worked so well that we adopted that tactic for all opposition thereafter.

We won by a goal in the end but it was as comfortable a three-point victory as you're likely to see. I had been substituted by the time the final whistle sounded but sprinted back on to join in the celebrations. I even jumped up on Brian Cody's back. Virtually anything goes in the 10-minute exemption period after an All-Ireland final. We've all seen Brian do his little jigs at the final whistle but he was always back to being the real Brian Cody by the time we returned to the dressing room after All-Ireland finals.

In the warm-up area he might address us and say something like, 'Well done, we did what we set out to do. Now go and enjoy your night.' Ned Quinn would sing 'The Rose of Mooncoin' and we'd form a huddle; Cody would participate without giving it his all. It just wasn't him.

It was a much-asked question after our various All-Ireland wins: how does this one compare? Many of the players said after the 2006 final that it was the most special and that still holds true for a lot of lads. If you look at 2006, it was a new Kilkenny team. A few of us, like Cha Fitzpatrick, Jackie Tyrrell and myself had been around for a year or two without making a real imprint. John Tennyson was a new centre-back. We stepped up as a team that day, beating a very seasoned Cork side with reasonable comfort, and maintained an incredibly high standard for years afterwards.

2011 would command a similar place in our affections. Tipperary were hailed as the coming force in the game after beating us in 2010. Although we had beaten them in 2009, we rode our luck before they turned us over the following year. Another defeat to them in 2011 would almost have been a de facto three-in-a-row for them and would have tarnished everything we'd done. That's the way we looked at it anyway. They'd shown some good form that year coming into the final and had put seven goals past Waterford. Ours was a more low key passage but we produced our best display in the final and beat them convincingly. That was sweet.

The Waterford game in 2008 was the greatest team performance I was ever involved in, finals or otherwise. I wasn't aware of just how well we were playing as the game was in progress and that's probably the key to why it was so good – if we had stopped to admire our work the final masterpiece mightn't have carried the same flourish.

I do remember a moment in the first half when we had established quite a lead and Ken McGrath, who was playing as a deep-lying centre-back, gesturing to Davy Fitzgerald as to whether he could go out and actually mark Henry Shefflin. Davy waved over with a firm 'no' and Ken was utterly demoralised. There was a bit of a bandwagon about Waterford in the run-up to that final and we used that to motivate ourselves. We certainly derailed it.

Jackie has explained how he got a thrill off dishing out hidings such as that and it's true, we did get a buzz from it, but for me it was more to do with us getting the very best out of ourselves. With most teams, once they establish a lead that appears to be unassailable, their intensity tends to drop quite noticeably but rarely with us. It was just down to our single-mindedness and a culture that we had developed as a group.

Brian was always keeping fellas on their toes by making changes from game to game and virtually nobody was safe. The dynamics within our panel were just perfect. We had up to 26 players who could slot in and it lent itself to every one of them maxing themselves out while they were on the field. And virtually every one of us was on song that day.

We did tend to go after goals more than most teams but I think the most critical difference in that respect was that if we went for a goal and it didn't come off, that was fine, we'd just keep going, whereas I felt it drained the opposition's confidence and energy when they butchered a goal chance.

That culture that I talk about was cultivated in Nowlan Park when we trained. To back up my point about how the drubbings we dished out were directly linked to the competition within the panel, you only have to look at how those type of comprehensive victories have become far less frequent over the past few years, even when we were still winning All-Irelands in 2014 and '15. That's because the savagery of the sessions wasn't quite the same from around 2011 or so.

You could say that the quality of player coming through wasn't as high but I felt that some of them could get to that level if they really wanted to, and that's where the frustration arose. It's not like every player that joined the panel a decade ago was ready-made and slotted in seamlessly to those training games; virtually nobody did. But they had the mental strength to drive it on and improve themselves, to reach the level of consistency required. That's what Kilkenny had lacked in the last few years.

At their peak, the training matches were just horrendous, and I mean that in the nicest possible way. It really steeled you for what was coming and, with all due respect, they were more testing than a lot of the championship games we played. In the early years, the games would go on for 60 minutes or so with no stoppages, other than a brief changeover at half-time. Cody would swallow the whistle and let us at it.

When there was a score or the ball went wide, there was a puckout straight away. If it went out for a sideline ball it was whipped back into play, so you were constantly on the go. It was relentless, but good for your conditioning and it toughened you up mentally. The players I'd mark most often in those games would be Tommy Walsh and JJ Delaney. Tommy was probably the best out and out hurler in the game but JJ was the best out and out defender; it was like he had about seven hands. Where's the respite there?

I held my own, otherwise I wouldn't have been selected as often as I was. Most of the duels would have been 50-50, or if someone got the better of you one particular night, you knew you had to return the compliment the next time. There was a live danger that you'd find yourself on the bench otherwise.

Aidan 'Taggy' Fogarty wouldn't be one of our most celebrated hurlers but he'd break Jackie's heart at times in those training games. Taggy was unorthodox and basically hit the ball all wrong. When he'd throw it up to strike, his left hand would then go to the top of the hurl to anchor it, something very few hurlers do. But his workrate more than satisfied Brian and he chipped in with plenty of scores too. He'd often take Jackie for seven or eight points in training.

'That's fucking it now, he's not hitting another ball off me again,' Jackie swore once. Then he went off and thought deeply about what Taggy was doing to get the better of him and concluded: 'I was trying to work it out for ages and it finally came to me – how the fuck was I going to work out what he was going to do with the ball when he didn't know what he was going to do with it himself?!'

The last of these training games would tend to take place on the Sunday before a championship match and as the years moved on they became shorter as sports science began to play more of a role and there was greater focus placed on recovery.

Sometimes the games boiled over, as you'd expect, and I was

at the centre of a particularly bizarre incident in the lead-up to the 2012 All-Ireland final replay against Galway. Pádraig Walsh was marking me and we got entangled at one stage and, before we knew it, we were wrestling on the ground. My helmet came off and the next thing I felt was a ferocious kick in the face which sent my head flying. It was big brother, Tommy Walsh. He could have broken my neck.

I absolutely lost the plot; just went nuts. I got up off the ground and started swinging my hurl like the grim reaper wielding his scythe as the lads pulled Tommy back. Matthew Ruth might have innocently got a good belt for his troubles. Cody came in and broke it all up but I was on my way.

'Fuck this, I'm not hanging around for this shit.'

Cody let a roar at me. I ignored him and kept going. He let another roar.

'What? Do you want me to stay for this fucking shit?'

'Come back here, come back,' he said.

I went back and finished out the last few minutes of training and then went straight in, got my clothes and headed for home without togging in. Anne's mother had been looking after the kids. My face had a big mark on it.

'Jesus, what happened to you?' she wondered.

'Ah, I got an oul belt in training.'

I got into the shower and was just coming out when the doorbell rang. Tommy.

'Jesus, Eoin, I don't know what came over me. I'm really sorry,' he said.

'Yeah, grand,' I said, as I slammed the door in his face.

Anne came home later. 'What happened your face?' 'Ah, I got an oul belt in training.' But she knew there was more to it than that. Later that night, when I'd calmed down a bit, I took out the phone and sent Tommy a text. 'Look, you did something wrong but you came up and apologised, we'll just forget about it now.'

The following day, a phone call from Anne. A now familiar question. 'What happened to your face?'

'I told you last night, I got a belt.'

'I know you didn't. Marlis is after texting me to say that Tommy gave you a boot in the face.'

'Sure how does she know?'

'Tommy told her. He feels brutal. She said he was beside himself last night.'

We moved past it fairly quickly. Tommy is one of my very best friends and Marlis, his wife, and Anne are close too. After we won the All-Ireland, we all had a great laugh about it in the pub. In fact, it was Tommy who put me up to singing from the Hogan Stand after I lifted the MacCarthy Cup that year. Donegal had won the football the previous Sunday and as I sat on the bus beside him that morning, I was humming that 'Jimmy's Winning Matches' tune.

'What's that?' Tommy said.

'Ah, it's that Donegal one…'

'Oh sing that,' he says, 'when we win today, sing that.'

I was looking down at him in the Hogan Stand later that day and he was nodding at me to do it. So I did. 'Cody's winning matches…' I don't exactly sing like a bird and got mercilessly slagged about it afterwards, but what harm? It was the only bum note from that day.

#########

I can remember going down to Kerry with my father, Allen, as a young lad. He'd borrow my aunt's red Ford Fiesta for the trip as he didn't have a car at the time. I would have been maybe seven or eight. On the way, he used to do this running commentary of me starring in an All-Ireland final and captaining Kilkenny to win. I used to get incredibly excited by the whole thing. He'd even be belting out Amhrán na bhFiann. He'd go full Roy of the Rovers on it. I was the youngest Kilkenny All-Ireland winning captain and I'd get the winning score in the final to boot. It didn't pan out quite like that in 2012 but it was close enough. 'Sing it again, Daddy,' I'd plead with him in the car. 'Sing it again.'

I was nominated to captain Kilkenny in 2012 by virtue of James Stephens winning the county title the year before. Lifting the Liam MacCarthy cup was just an unbelievable feeling. It was something I had dreamed about, like any young lad, since I was a child. Ellie was little more than a year old at that stage and I got a much-treasured picture with her on the field as well as Mark and Holly too after the game. Ellie was small enough to slot into the cup.

My father never used to go to the post-match banquet in Citywest, but he did in 2012. 'Sing it again,' he said to me that night. No explanation was needed. It was more of the same in The Village Inn the following night when, full as a tick, he was really emotional, tears flowing.

Even now, if there's a picture produced of me with the cup, he'll throw it out.

'Sing it again.'

#########

Saturday, September 8, 2018

My family tree isn't exactly a conventional one. But then, what is a conventional family these days? My parents' marriage broke up when I was quite young. Both remarried and had further children with their new spouses. That left me with two brothers and a sister. Or so I thought.

A few years back my father told me that he had another daughter, long before he met my mother, Lucy. He'd been seeing a girl and she fell pregnant. They were both quite young and, back in 1970s Ireland, keeping the child wasn't a realistic option. Their daughter was put up for adoption. I'm sketchy on the details as, naturally enough, it isn't my father's favourite topic though I do know that he went out to the hospital to see them a couple of days after she was born but they were gone. And that was it. He never got to hold his baby daughter. He got on with his life but always carried a certain sort of guilt over it.

It was only about four or five years ago that he told me about her. Of course, I was curious about it but somewhat reluctant to make contact. So many questions. Where would it go? Is that what she'd want? Would it be upsetting the life she now has? I had a lot going on. I was still hurling for Kilkenny and had a young family. I let it drift to the back of my mind but it occupied my thoughts more frequently once I retired.

Funnily enough, my father was in contact with her through Facebook but hadn't met her. He was afraid to. They'd exchange messages here and there and he'd sometimes show me a photo of her. Her name was Kim.

The summer of 2018 proved to be the catalyst for things

finally moving beyond that. I got tickets for the Munster football final between Cork and Kerry down in Páirc Uí Chaoimh and was going down with my father and a friend. Kim lives in Cork so, being down there, it got me thinking about her. We had a few pints after the game and on the way back up I got stuck into my father about not having met her.

'Ah sure if she wanted that she'd get on to me.'

'What age are you?' I fired back. 'You're not seven anymore waiting for your friend to call over!'

'Ah well, it's difficult, it's difficult…'

So I thought to myself, *fuck this, I'm not waiting around for him to make a move on it.* I took out the phone and shot her a message. It went from there. We exchanged messages for a couple of weeks and tiptoed around the elephant in the room until I finally blurted it out: 'Look, I'd love to meet you but I understand if you don't want to, there's absolutely no pressure.' She immediately said that she'd love to. 'I'm glad one of us worked up the courage to ask!' she said.

Today, we met for the first time. I drove down to her home in Cork with Anne and the three kids. I was fairly relaxed about it, and quite excited actually, though Anne was nervous on the way down. I suppose she just really wanted things to work out for me. We pulled up at the house and her husband, Khaled, came out to meet us. I had a bunch of flowers. 'They're not for you, now,' I laughed.

When Kim came out, we just shook hands and exchanged pleasantries.

We went inside, there was a platter of sandwiches produced and we drank coffee and talked. I wouldn't say it was awkward initially but I wouldn't say it wasn't awkward either. What do we talk about? Does she want to get into it about my father and everything that went before? You're feeling in the dark a bit really, and it's surreal meeting your sister for the first time at 34 years of age. Khaled broke the ice.

'I can see a bit of a resemblance with the two of you,' he said, and from there the conversation took on a life of its own.

They have four daughters and their youngest girl, Leah, was asleep on the couch. I noted how she looked just like my aunt from a picture my father had shown me of her when she was that age. Kim told me about her adopted family. She has one other sister but her father, to whom she was particularly close, had died a few years earlier while she was living in Dubai. It was nice that she felt comfortable enough to talk to me in detail about things like that having just met. Later, we all went out for a walk by the river. Kim has four young daughters and they hit it off with our kids pretty well as they went pottering about together.

You'd ask yourself why you waited so long to reach out to someone like this. But then she had been living overseas for a few years and I had a lot going on between hurling and family. I wouldn't have had the time to put into this relationship that I do now. As it was, it took me long enough to pluck up the courage just to ask her to meet up at this stage of my life. I most certainly wouldn't have been able to summon that courage when I was a younger man.

Kim's philosophical about how things played out with her being adopted. She's a very positive person and carries no grudges. She's happy with her lot.

'Eoin, everything happens for a reason,' she told me.

In all, we spent about six hours with them before heading

for home. The whole experience was brilliant, to be honest. I was absolutely delighted with how it went. As we left, Kim and I embraced warmly this time and loosely agreed to meet up again soon.

September has given me so many great moments and memories to look back on. Now it's given me more that I can look forward to.

#########

In my childhood and adolescence, it wasn't only September that was contaminated by the fact that I would be going back to school. It seeped into August, too. That's when the 'back to school' signs would start to appear in the shops. The end of the summer holidays was when the fear would really start to grip me. I couldn't even enjoy the last week of the holidays because the thoughts of returning to school would plague me. I absolutely hated school. Although I never mitched or anything like that, my motivation for going to school was zero. It had nothing to do with being academically bright or otherwise, I just wanted to be anywhere but there.

I attended St Patrick's De La Salle for primary school and had a couple of teachers who would be at the coalface during my Kilkenny career. It wasn't all plain sailing with Paul Kinsella, who taught me in fifth class and would later go on to be county board chairman. He said something to me one day that wasn't to my liking – though I can't recall what it was – so I marched out of the school and all the way down to my father's workplace. He came back up and spoke to Paul outside the classroom and there was never any hassle again.

To be fair, I had a great relationship with Paul when he was chairman, as I did with everyone on the county board.

Come sixth class my teacher was one Brian Cody. I looked up to him. Back then, he was the man who managed the James Stephens senior hurling team, which was everything, but he had apparently captained Kilkenny to an All-Ireland before I was born. Certainly not a bad back catalogue, even if his greatest compositions were still to come. So he carried a reputation. A reputation for being a scary man if he started shouting at you. He had this throaty roar that I heard all too often through both academia and hurling. 'LARKEEEGGHH!', with the characteristic 'gghh' always tailing it off at the end.

Of course, he had ways of dealing with people that traversed both the classroom and dressing room but he wouldn't be as cut-throat with his students as he was with hurlers.

As a player in later years, many's the time he'd tell me, straight out, that I was fat. Once, in Carton House, our nutritionist was going through my diet and weight with me just as Brian was walking by. 'I'm happy enough with that,' she says. 'Noreen, he's fat,' he says to her. I reasoned that I had ticked all the boxes and had been up on the scales.

'You're fat. You've a big fat arse on you.' He'd say it in a humorous fashion but the message was clear – you better get rid of it. I had that type of conversation with him about my weight several times over the years.

He knew he couldn't be that blunt with his students. I remember one classmate, a real messer, that he lost the plot with a number of times. He came from a very difficult background, with both of his parents alcoholics, so the story went. Because of that, Brian gave him every chance but he'd always pull some stroke to annoy him. He'd get that roar on a regular basis but it was always forgotten about the next day. You knew that, under it all, Brian was quite fond of him and wanted him to succeed in spite of what he was going home to every day. It's hardly a coincidence that after primary school, when he probably didn't have a figure like that looking out for him, he really went off the rails, later becoming a heroin addict and having a number of stretches in jail.

I found school more tolerable when under Brian's tutelage, though that was probably more down to the fact that we used to go out and play hurling a fair bit than for academic reasons, even if he was a good teacher. The lads in the Kilkenny panel would always chide me that I was his pet and, when he taught me, I would have got the feeling that, basically, he liked me. He picked me on the school teams and even made me captain, which was a great boon to my confidence at that age.

Come secondary school, I had to peel myself out of the bed every morning and I'd literally count the minutes until each class would end. I spent three years in St Kieran's College, the famous nursery of Kilkenny hurling, but they all meshed into one monotonous countdown. Using my time in the school to develop myself as a hurler and ultimately win the Dr Croke Cup wasn't any great incentive. I put in a big effort hurling-wise when I started there with the under-14 team and, under Séamus Knox and Tom Hogan, I was exposed to real physical work for the first time. I bought into it but then I didn't make the team. I went through a phase then whereby my interest in hurling was waning though I still used it to get off classes if I could.

I would have applied myself somewhat for practical subjects like technology and I wanted to do woodwork but Kieran's didn't offer it at the time. Certain parts of biology intrigued me but that was it. In a bid to cajole me into becoming something more studious, my parents enrolled me in after-school study in Kieran's from 6pm-10pm but it was so long that I'd just do my homework and then fall asleep. I eventually refused to go but ended up in a shorter study session though I barely lifted a finger there either.

I told my parents that I would sit my Junior Cert and then that would be it, I was leaving school. They insisted I'd have to go out and work. 'Fine,' I said. I did ok in my exams and was pleasantly surprised because I had done no study whatsoever. None. I couldn't get the uniform off quickly enough after I sat my last exam. Finished with school and not yet 16 years old. I later came to regret that and would absolutely not want it for our children.

It certainly didn't help fast-track my Kilkenny career. Quite the opposite, in fact. I didn't make the Kilkenny minor panel until halfway through my final year of eligibility. The manager was Nicky Cashin, a teacher in Kieran's, and my leaving school certainly wouldn't have pushed me up the pecking order.

I played a game for the club minor team against Johnstown one evening and hit eight or nine points from play. Apparently Joe Hennessy and Brian Cody went to Cashin afterwards and asked him if there was a better minor in the county. I was eventually added to the panel ahead of the All-Ireland semi-final against Galway which we won before beating Tipperary in the final, though I didn't feature at all.

The medal that I got meant little to me though the experience drove me and, on reflection, it was a huge factor in my subsequent progress. Kilkenny won the senior title the same day and being wrapped up in all of that fuelled me with motivation. I was determined that I wouldn't be a sub picking up a handy medal again.

#########

Now, with my Kilkenny days behind me, September has come full circle again. It means trying to get the kids organised for school. It means expense. Uniforms, books, stationery costs at the school. Anne always gets stressed out about it. 'Do I have everything? I don't want them to be without anything.' It was even worse for her when I'd be building up to playing in an All-Ireland final, ridding myself of any distractions. To be fair, if it wasn't for her they'd be going in without a scrap as they wouldn't want to be relying on me to be organised.

In time, September will come to mean them going off to college, something I wouldn't think about too often though sometimes we wonder, 'How are we going to afford them going to college if this is what it's costing for them to go to school?' It's a few years away yet, though. Mark, the eldest, is into school and is now in Kieran's himself so I'd imagine college is something he'll want to do.

Holly seemed to be every inch my daughter when in primary school, as she didn't like it at all. I thought we'd have to be pushing her every bit of the way. Now, since she went into first year in secondary school, she loves it and draws up study plans and all sorts. She aspires to be a vet, for now.

Ellie had just gone four when she started school so we opted to keep her back in first class in 2018, something that I had gone through myself having done fifth class twice. It's been brilliant for her. The extra year made a huge difference. Flying through all her work and a great help to her classmates with their lessons. Not quite a chip off the old block!

#########

The greater the distance from my Kilkenny career, the more its relevance diminishes. I've got more than half my life ahead of me, I hope, and in that context my playing days will find their place. Maybe I'm wrong, but I can't help thinking that once you finish playing, people just forget about it. The eight All-Ireland medals are great to have but they're decreasingly important in my life now as it moves forward. They're in a box in my mother's attic. There's not much in our home that would tell you I played for Kilkenny if you didn't already know.

You might think, what's the point in doing it so? Well, I did it because I thoroughly enjoyed it at that time. I would never play down how fortunate I was to have hurled for Kilkenny in the era that I did and to have enjoyed so many great days. I was lucky in that my career coincided with a time when sports science was more de rigeur and greater emphasis was placed on recovery and such things. But I didn't escape unscathed.

I had hip surgery when I was 25 and was told I'd probably get another 15 years out of that joint before it would need to be replaced. That's creeping ever closer. When you're lying on a hospital bed after getting your hip done, you're not thinking,

'I'll be grand, sure I've eight All-Ireland medals.' Look at Darach Honan having to retire early with a hip problem due to overtraining and the Clare county board telling him where to go when it came to covering the cost of the surgery. I don't worry about what's around the corner in that respect but Anne does. The prospect of wheeling me around isn't terribly appealing!

Would I do it all again? Absolutely. Though I'm not sure that I could devote myself to anything like the same degree again, and that's not necessarily a bad thing either because, at times, it just wasn't healthy.

Everything went into it. As I've said, there were episodes over the years when Brian Cody would have pointed out that I wasn't in the shape that I needed to be in. I'd have tried to do all the right things with my diet and training but when the weight wasn't dropping to the extent that it needed to, the lecture would come. Sometimes it would be a question that left room for one answer only: 'Do you think you're in good physical shape?'

At that, I'd basically just stop eating. I could eat a banana, have three or four cups of coffee over the course of the day, hit the gym for an hour, go for a run in the evening. I'd be obsessive that way. I might treat myself to a second banana or an apple but that'd be it for the day. Is that healthy?

But my hurling career, for now at least, can still open doors for me. It's up to me then whether I decide to go through those doors and make the best of whatever opportunity is on the other side.

Having a few All-Ireland medals won't carry you too far, and rightly so.

Friday, September 28, 2018

I completed my first week's work today in my new job with TransferMate Global Payments, an international payments company which is based in Kilkenny. Having left the Defence Forces, I had been working in Pfizer in Saggart since January of last year. The work itself was fine but I had grown weary of the travel and the shifts and was on the lookout for something different.

I ran into my cousin, Nigel Donovan, while in The Steppes Bar in Callan a few weeks ago. He works for Taxback, a sister company to TransferMate, and I asked him if there were any jobs going. 'I don't think we're looking for anyone in Taxback, but I think there could be a few going in TransferMate,' he said. 'Leave it with me and I'll see.' TransferMate is essentially a middle man when it comes to making international payments. If a person or company are buying something in, say, pounds sterling, they can pay TransferMate in euro and they'll then make a payment to the other party from our sterling account.

In fairness to Nigel, things moved pretty swiftly from there. A chap called Cathal Ryan, who works in human resources for TransferMate, gave me a call to come in for an interview for the post of business development manager.

Hurling often weaves its way through the narrative in things I do and it was very much the case throughout this process, right through to my starting the job this week. Cathal used to hurl for Johnstown so we chatted a bit about the club championship as well.

When the interview came round, he was joined by Tom

Butler, the main man in the company, who's from Waterford but lives in Wexford.

'I hate Kilkenny!' he laughed as he began. It was an ice-breaker and the conversation veered between hurling and the job over the course of the interview. He'd ask about Brian Cody and things like that. 'I admire all the things you did with Kilkenny, apart from 2008. You just had that drive and it's very evident that it's still there.' But the fact that I had no background in this line of work was a concern for him, understandably so.

'You've no sales experience, what if I give you this job?' he wondered.

'Well Tom, I didn't have any pharmaceutical experience when I went to Pfizer either, but I gained it.'

'Yeah, fair point, fair point.'

Tom conducted the interview in a very pleasant fashion, I have to say. There was hurling talk and then he'd get serious and draw it back to the job, before reverting to hurling again. It helped put me at ease. A few days later Cathal called and offered me the job. Naturally, I was delighted.

Did my hurling background help me get the job? I would say so, yes, because my lack of experience in this field was clearly an issue for Tom, but I think the drive that he saw in me compensated for that.

On the other hand, if I went in for that interview with a nonchalance about me because I had a few All-Ireland medals, I absolutely would not have got the job. Tom would see right through that. Humility was a feature of our Kilkenny team and lads that lacked that quality didn't last very long. You had to respect the jersey and what it's about and conduct yourself in a certain way off the field as well. That's something that's stood to me outside of hurling. While what I did on the field won't put food on the table, it can help me without being exploited in a cynical manner.

On my first day last Monday, I was given a desk beside Cathal Dunne, someone I'd never spoken to before, yet I knew him through hurling. He'd be a few years older than me but had played for Graiguenamanagh and at underage for Kilkenny and was fairly handy. So you can guess what we started talking about once we were properly introduced. I've been given a list of potential clients to try and develop. But it's not a finite list, so what do I? Delve into my hurling contacts, which throws up one or two leads.

It was a good first week. It's a totally different challenge for me and one that, 10 years ago, might have been too much for me to take on. I would probably have lacked the confidence and resilience to do something like that back then.

2

OCTOBER

*'You're just going to have to wait until I'm
playing to win one!'*

Though names and faces change over time, every club tends to have certain characteristics and traits that bind the generations. With James Stephens, some of those have probably been diluted in recent times but one thing I would still go back to is our pride. It's something we often speak about, the colours we wear, what it means and how lucky we are to represent the club. 'Look at the jersey you're wearing and look at the jersey you're playing against – there's no comparison,' is a familiar refrain from our dressing room. We're known as 'The Village' despite hailing from the Patrick Street area of Kilkenny city.

When I look back, I would say that we've produced largely skilful players for Kilkenny. Joe Hennessy and Liam 'Chunky' O'Brien would fit into that category. Brian Cody too. Philly

Larkin and Brian McEvoy the same. Then the likes of Fan Larkin, Peter Barry and Jackie Tyrrell would have mixed their skill with a hard edge. Tough men. I wouldn't class myself as a hard man but I'd be satisfied that my stickwork is of a high standard. Even now, Luke Scanlon and Conor Browne carry many of the same traits.

The club's history, which included All-Ireland club titles in 1976 and '82, would infuse you with confidence growing up. When I was a young lad, one of the junior hurlers gave my father a pair of club socks that were too small for him and he passed them on to me. They were red with a green stripe and when wearing them I felt like could have done anything with a hurl in my hand. I wore them out and even at that, I still kept wearing them for ages.

Michael 'Sla' Slattery and Seán Brennan were among the predominant underage mentors in the club when I was starting out. They would go to extraordinary lengths for us. For the finals of the underage leagues in the club, we'd be paraded around the field and Seán would have a stereo up on his shoulder blasting out the tunes, with Amhrán na bhFiann to round it all off. It felt like a massive occasion when you were that age.

The Larkin name is one that's synonymous with the club, though largely from another leg of the family. Fan, who emulated his father Paddy by winning All-Irelands with Kilkenny, is my father's first cousin. Paddy and my grandfather, Ned, were brothers. Ned was called in to hurl for Kilkenny but only went to one training session. 'I'm not going in to hurl with them country fellas,' he declared afterwards.

Fan used to give me a hard time as a young lad because of

how I held the hurl. I'm left-handed so I was just doing what came naturally to me. No matter to Fan. 'You're holding the hurl the wrong way!' he'd bark. He'd cause me to try it the other way though after a few minutes I'd revert. But for years he'd still bang on at me about it.

Then he'd tell me that I was too fond of hitting the ball on the one side all the time. Funnily enough, though I'm left-handed, my stronger side is my right but then I'd try hitting it on my left and, again, would give up after a few minutes, like most young lads who just don't want to do something that they're not good at. But Fan was right and I had to put a lot of work into my left side in my late teens to get it up to standard, even though it's still only about 75 percent of what my right is. I'd strike the ball the same distance on either side but am more accurate off my right.

As I gathered All-Ireland medals, my father would always reference it in the context of Fan. 'You've the same amount as Fan now...' 'You've one more than Fan now...' My father and Fan would often drink together in The Village Inn. 'Jaysus, TJ had a great game today,' my father might say. 'Ah, I thought he was poor, I thought he was poor,' Fan would reply, just for devilment. That's the sort of character he is.

Fan's a legend in the game but I never saw him play so it's much less tangible for me. It was different with his son, Philly, who carried on the tradition with club and county and was someone I naturally looked up to. Although he wasn't in my immediate family, it still gave me belief that a Larkin was doing it at the highest level. I'd have been in awe of him a little, if I'm honest. It wasn't just because of the blood lines either. It was the type of character he was. I remember one club match against Dunamaggin in Thomastown years ago, he was playing centre-back and it was like a tennis rally between him and the opposition. He'd catch the ball and drive it down the field, catch the subsequent clearance, back down again and so on. Warrior-like.

At the All-Ireland under-21 final against Galway in Tullamore in 1994, he got his teeth knocked out after a row broke out during the parade. He had false ones after that but they always came out on match day. When I played with him, I remember him marching around the dressing room. Wired. No front teeth. At the top of his game, he was always like that. Driven. No one could talk to him. It'd get you in the mood fairly sharp.

It's the sort of thing I feel we've missed at senior level in recent years. That take-no-shit demeanour. We have players that would hurl the ears off you but we've lacked that hard edge and other teams have picked up on it and fed off it. We don't carry a fear factor that we might have historically. We're looked on as soft city lads now. And I rail against that perception. But the only place we can change it is on the field.

Saturday, October 6, 2018

We didn't do that today, but at least we're still alive after drawing the county quarter-final against Erin's Own, Castlecomer. We were steeped. I don't think any of us could walk off the field saying we won our individual duel, myself very much included.

I had the build-up from hell, though. I was in tremendous pain with my neck all week and after dry needles, an injection and anti-inflammatories it finally settled down a bit last night. I had a peritrostomy procedure on my hip in 2009 but it still bothers me in that I get a soreness between my groin and hamstring. I have a routine of getting a needle in my groin a few days before games to bring some relief but, due to my neck issues, I only get it done last night and it hadn't settled down in time for today's game. It bothered me throughout the match and Conor Delaney dominated me.

This year, I've played at midfield with a view to dropping back and helping the defence after the goals we shipped to Dicksboro in last year's county final but then I was moved to centre-forward today. I found that a little odd given that, as our first knockout fixture, it was our most important game of the year so far.

Castlecomer were five points clear but they seemed to panic and we somehow got a draw out of it. I scored the equalising point, and there was some satisfaction in that, particularly with how we worked the ball cleverly and calmly up the field. Last year we might have been more likely to balloon it out of defence.

But we got away with it against a team that we should be beating without too much fuss. Here's hoping we've heeded the lessons and will do just that in the replay.

##########

Sunday, October 14, 2018

The Village stereotype was reinforced yesterday in Ballyragget. Beaten by two points in the replay and we could have no complaints. It's absolutely heartbreaking. I questioned during the week why I was moved to centre-forward and ended up back in midfield yesterday but game plans and formations had little to do with it.

When I first came into The Village senior team we weren't short on leaders but once some of the more established lads finished up, I felt too much of the responsibility to drive the thing on rested on the likes of Jackie, Matthew Ruth and myself; the county players. We were absolutely destroyed by Mullinavat earlier in the year and Jackie said to me afterwards, 'I was so looking forward to just going out and hurling this year and letting everyone else drive it on but it doesn't look like it's going to happen.'

We got it together after that and won the league but once it came to the real knockout hurling in the championship, we fell flat again. I'm 34, Jackie's 36 and we just don't have it in the legs to get around the pitch like we used to. At his peak, Jackie would nearly be hurling the six positions at the back. We need others to pick up the mantle but, for some reason, it's just not happening. And the most frustrating thing is that we have plenty of hurlers with the ability.

It was nip and tuck in the first half but they just got ahead of us before half-time and we were chasing them for most of the second half. I started the game well but I got knocked out cold midway through the first half and wasn't quite the same after it. I went to collect a short puckout and turned around to a shoulder straight in the face. The same player should already have been sent off for pulling across Conor Browne's faceguard, but he didn't even get booked, and he only got a yellow for the challenge on me.

When I came to I was hit with questions from the medical team asking me where I was, who were we playing and who got the last point. I answered them all and got up and played on but there was blood spilling out of my lip and into the chin of my faceguard. I went out of it till half-time but improved in the second half, I felt. We actually managed to get ahead coming down the home straight after scoring a penalty but they still drove on to win.

I was just numb at the final whistle. We're better than them, yet we allowed the game to be played on their terms. Out-muscled. Bullied. Same old shit. If we could have gotten over this I'd have fancied ourselves against Ballyhale Shamrocks in the semi. I'm sure if we got them in Nowlan Park we would have won but we get dragged down to their level in places like Ballyragget. We just let teams do that to us.

Did I do enough myself? Absolutely not and I'll be the first to admit that. At half-time I had a go at Niall Brassil, a young player who's a terrific prospect. 'You need to up your work rate,' I told him, 'you're our best player and you haven't done a tap. People are talking about you for Kilkenny next year, come on.' Peter Barry, who's a selector, ushered me away. The word I'm hearing around the club since is that I was too hard on Brazzo. Maybe I was. It was just in the heat of the moment. I just want the club to do well and for Niall to do himself justice.

I couldn't get out of the dressing room quickly enough afterwards. The usual end of year speeches were going on. Niall Tyrrell announced that he'd be stepping down. The chairman said his few words. You had the ripples of applause and that was it, another opportunity squandered.

After the belt I got, I was feeling shit – even more than I had been – on the drive home. Blinding headache. I was thinking of going to the hospital but I just couldn't move. I hit the couch and didn't get off it until 10 o'clock. Wiped out. Fell asleep. I perked up then and had a few bottles over at my cousin's house-warming across the road in Callan.

There would be others in the club that would share my view and then some others that wouldn't. This weekend for the club was best summed up by an exchange a friend of mine had with the Comer management during our game yesterday. Their selector told him to get off the field.

'Come over and make me. You're too soft to fucking come over.'

'All your soft lads are out on the field,' came the reply.

He told me, 'Sure, fuck him, I couldn't say anything after that. I had to shut me mouth. The c**t was right.'

#########

The upshot of us losing is that I got to see Kim again sooner than I thought I would. Her husband, Khaled, who is Lebanese, was keen on seeing me play so if we got through to the semi-final they were all going to come up for it next weekend. If we lost yesterday they'd come up today instead, which is what they did. They were a bit late as Leah, their youngest girl, was unwell so we didn't go to the Castle Park or the bowling alley as we had planned. They came to my father's house, him finally having gone and met her a few weeks ago.

'Well, how did you get on?' I asked him at the time.

'Jesus, great. We had a great day.'

'You see, it wasn't rocket science, all you had to do was reach out.'

'Ah I know,' he said, 'but there's a lot of guilt there.'

'But I told you, she doesn't hold anything like that. She's just positive about everything.'

'I know, I know, I know…thanks.'

In the few weeks since Kim and I first met, I've been in contact with her quite a lot through text. Just regular stuff like how each other's day is going and stuff about our families largely, building the relationship bit by bit, catching up on the decades we've missed out on and covering the ground quite quickly, in fairness. So quickly, in fact, that we've effectively got all the mushy shit out of the way. I told her that, from here on, she'll always be part of our family. She responded in kind and told me how glad she was that I had made contact.

When they arrived today, Kim and I embraced and I gave her a kiss on the cheek. There was nothing contrived or awkward about it.

I showed her around. The joke in the family is that my father's home is something of a shrine to me. He would have bought photographs from my Kilkenny career from Sportsfile and had them framed for the hall and sitting room. We sat down then and had a cup of tea. Kim has quite the Cork accent, which is a bit surreal when you think about it, though she's not into the GAA at all. She certainly wasn't in Croke Park roaring for the Rebels when I was playing against them!

We had booked a table in Langton's for the whole lot of us, my family, my father's family and Kim's, so we walked down that far then. It was a case of leaping into the unknown the first time we met but all of those inhibitions are gone now and we all chat freely over dinner as I, freed from any dietary constraints after yesterday's exit, devoured a burger and apple crumble.

Still though, you'd think of what we've missed out on together, things we won't get back. All of the rest of my family were there for all of the All-Irelands I won. You remember the embraces when you first see them after the final whistle. She could have been part of all that and it is something that I thought about coming towards the end of my career.

It adds another layer of disappointment to us being beaten yesterday.

I had allowed myself to think ahead to us winning the county final and being out on the field after the final whistle. My father coming down. My mother coming down. Anne and the kids coming down. Louise coming down. Anthony coming down. Allen Junior coming down. And Kim coming down.

Sharing that kind of moment with her as I had with the rest of them so many times over the years. Hopefully we'll get that chance yet.

We went back to my father's after Langton's for a while before Kim and her family headed for home. We embraced warmly again before she left.

We may have missed out on a lot together but there's no doubt about it now, she's my sister.

I now have two brothers and two sisters, and don't differentiate between any of them.

##########

Tuesday, October 17, 2018

The disappointment really took hold of me today, three days after our championship exit. I went off to work as normal on Monday and dealt with the inevitable chit-chat around our game without too much difficulty. 'Yeah, look, we just weren't good enough, no complaints.' But after I got in yesterday morning I began thinking about the loss more and more, churning it around in my head. I hadn't spoken to Cathal Ryan on Monday, he works upstairs, so when he popped over to my desk I knew he only had one thing in mind. 'Don't start,' I said to him, kind of joking, kind of abrupt. 'Fair enough. I'll come back to you around Thursday or Friday so.' I went upstairs later and had a chat with him about it. I was like a demon, though.

To be honest, on the way home from Ballyragget on Saturday I felt like pulling the car in and just having a good cry. But I couldn't do that. There'd be a cavalcade from the club coming behind me and I didn't want them to see me blubbing on the hard shoulder, then pulling in to check if I was alright. I thought I had processed that part of it but in work yesterday I had this knot in my stomach and just wanted to go away into a corner and bawl my eyes out.

It's not something I've done very often, but it has happened on occasions after traumatic defeats. The most obvious one is the 2010 All-Ireland final. After losing the final, you're still together as a group for a few days after, numb from the drink. But when real life kicks back in and you go back to work, that's when it really hits you. About a week after Tipperary beat us, I just took myself off in the car, pulled in and had a good cry.

I made sure to stay out long enough so that the redness had cleared from my eyes when I got home. Anne has barely ever seen me cry in all the years we've been together.

I did it after last year's county final defeat. And after the 2009 county final loss I was moving from one pub to another with Anne and a crew when the tears just started streaming down my cheeks. In the end, I didn't cry yesterday, reasoning that if I tried to disappear after work for a while, she'd wonder what had kept me. So I bottled it up. She knew there was something up with me when I got home last night all the same.

'You're snappy, you're not yourself.'

'What are you talking about? I'm grand.'

Tomorrow should be easier though. The job is going well and, when the fog of this loss clears, I'll appreciate things like that more.

#########

Sunday, October 21, 2018

I was on my bed watching Manchester United get pinned back for a 2-2 draw with Chelsea on the iPad yesterday when the phone rang.

It was Joe Malone, who used to be a masseur with the Kilkenny team and is now a local Fianna Fáil councillor. I helped him out with a bit of canvassing in the past. Ahead of the 2009 local elections, Kilkenny were gunning for four-in-a-row, I was reigning Hurler of the Year and I suppose he concluded that my face wasn't going to do him any harm on the doorsteps. I assumed that that was what he was calling about again as I answered.

'Look, I'm going to ask you something and you can tell me to fuck off if you want,' he began. 'I'd prefer to do it face-to-face but I'm going to say it to you anyway: there's an election on next year, would you be interested in running for Fianna Fáil?'

He completely caught me on the hop. I went quiet for a few seconds before finally blurting out: 'Jaysus Joe, you're after catching me out there. I didn't expect that, I'm nearly after falling off the bed!'

Joe was cute enough to keep the prospect alive, however. 'Don't say no now,' he said. 'Have a think about it, if you want to meet me this evening or tomorrow I'll explain it.'

So I met him in the Aspect Hotel yesterday evening and he ran me through the ins and outs of it. The election will be next May. He reckons there'll be six seats for the taking in my electoral area, five of which Fianna Fáil should have pretty much sewn up already. That's where I'd come in. I tick a lot of boxes in that even though I come from 'The Village' area of the city, I now live out in Callan, where I also have a lot of relatives, and all of that falls within the catchment area.

'You're well known, you're liked in the Village, you're living in Callan, you know a good few people out there,' Joe said. 'I know Cody's Fine Gael, but I'd say he'd give you a vote. You mightn't get number one but you'd probably get number two!'

'Give it two or three weeks and have a think about,' he added. 'If you don't want to do it, you don't want to do it. There'll be no hard feelings.'

So I told him I'd have a think about it. Although I canvassed with him in the past, it wasn't on a large scale and I'm not big into politics. The presidential election is in full swing at the moment but I have no interest and doubt if I'll even bother voting next Friday. Politics wouldn't have been a big thing in our family either but we'd be more aligned to Fianna Fáil than any other party. I'd give Sinn Féin the odd vote as well.

When I threw it out to the family, I didn't get quite the reaction I was expecting. I thought my father, and others, would ask me if I was mad and tell me to cop myself on for even considering it. But he didn't. Now, he didn't actively encourage me to do it either but the fact that he laughed at the good of it and didn't shoot it down was more positivity than I had been counting on from him. My mother was supportive and Anne's parents, Pat and Anne, who would be more staunch Fianna Fáil, were particularly so.

It's something that Anne and I would have to sit down and discuss in more detail but she's certainly not against it. We have three young children and the extra money that it would bring in on top of our wages is not to be sneezed at. I know you shouldn't get involved in politics for that reason though anyone who says it isn't a factor on some level is full of shit. But I'm still so wrapped up in hurling that something would have to give somewhere along the line.

In light of the encouragement I've received, I'm warming to the idea, even if the prospect of seeing my face on posters and the possibility of being called 'Councillor Eoin Larkin' makes me a little squeamish – and wide open for unmerciful slagging!

When I think about it, certain aspects of it do appeal to me. My own parents had to source different living arrangements after their marriage broke down and I'd like to be able to help people who find themselves in a somewhat similar position, looking for a council house, say. Or pushing for funding for a playground in the area I'm living in now. Getting involved in things like that excites me a little. I'd want to show people that I'm more than just a lad who got elected on the back of winning a few All-Irelands.

Everyone suffered to some degree during the recession and I certainly wasn't immune to it. In 2009, I went to do a non-commissioned officer (NCO) course in Cork. It lasts a few months and when you get back, you're automatically promoted. I was 10 weeks into it when an embargo on promotions was announced. I had to wait four years, while my wages were cut too, leaving me down about €120 a week at a time when we had two small children and Anne wasn't working.

We were conscientious, though. We had a mortgage at the time and never got caught up in the extravagance that marked the Celtic Tiger years. I was always brought up to pay your bills and live off whatever you have left after that. If that meant you had to miss out on certain things, then tough. I used to find that frustrating with my mother, but it stood to me big time and Anne is of a similar outlook.

People got themselves into a lot of bother during the boom, when everything seemed to be on the never never. Throw it on the credit card. If that's maxed out, get another one and if you need a holiday, go to the bank and they'll give you the money. You had 100 percent mortgages; I went on a tour of duty overseas to ensure that I had a deposit for a house. It was very frustrating that we didn't live anything even remotely close to a champagne lifestyle and we still paid quite a price. But I would direct my ire more at the banks than any political party or politician for that.

Issues like this are commanding an increasing presence in my thoughts on the back of Joe's approach. Fleetingly, you jump ahead and think that if you got elected to the council and it went well, it might lead to bigger things. 'You're looking at the next TD for Carlow-Kilkenny!' I joked to my father. But, first things first, I have a lot of thinking to do over the next few weeks.

##########

Sunday, October 28, 2018

My sister, Louise, ran in the Dublin City Marathon today. She was always there to support me on my biggest days in hurling. She would be one of the first out on the field after a game and now it was time to be there for her.

She was never particularly sporty and only took up running a couple of years ago. She joined Fit For Life in Kilkenny and went from there. She wouldn't have been able to do a lap of the track when she started without stopping and look at her now. She's lost a fair bit of weight, her self-esteem has improved and socially it's been very good for her too.

I'm more than four years years older than her. We grew up in the same house and, in fairness, her father, Paddy, never treated her any differently to me because I was his stepson. While Louise and I had our moments when growing up, we've always got on well. Since I moved out of the house, I don't think we've had a single argument and she's very good to the kids.

When she finished school, I pleaded with her to go to college, drawing on my own personal experience, but she insisted on taking a year out first and, of course, she didn't follow through on my advice. However, she later did all the childcare courses and loves working in that field now.

She was to start the marathon at around 9.45am so we left shortly after 10, planning to get to the cheering area on mile 22. We did a bit of shopping in Dundrum first and Anne was following her progress through the app on the phone and we appeared to be in plenty of time. But we discovered that the app only updates on a staggered basis and she had passed the cheering area by the time we got there. We scampered to try and catch up with her and ended up getting a taxi to the finishing line at Merrion Square. My mother got to her first and reached across the rails to hug her before myself, Anne and Holly joined in. She was in floods of tears.

'Ye weren't at mile 22 and I started bawling when I didn't see you,' she said.

I felt really guilty then because I can imagine how someone could be flagging at that stage of a marathon and seeing your family and them egging you on would surely give you a huge lift. She was a little disappointed with her time but she had been suffering with the 'flu a few days beforehand.

'You came to so many of my matches and supported me throughout my career, it was great to just be there for something you wanted to do,' I told her proudly at the finish line.

That the marathon fell on county final day in Kilkenny

was also a handy excuse to be well away from Nowlan Park. Another title for Ballyhale Shamrocks.

##########

County finals have been very much a mixed bag for me. Played six, won three, lost three. I suppose if you looked at it a certain way, you could take some comfort in the fact that we've been competing regularly at the business end of the championship and winning a few of them, even though I believe we could and should have won more.

From 1981 to 2004, the Tom Walsh Cup never came to The Village. Getting to the final was largely beyond us too. There were a couple of years where we lost semi-finals to Fenians out in Ballyragget, reinforcing the stereotype of townies struggling in tighter surrounds. Then the 1996 semi-final against Fenians was fixed for Nowlan Park and we beat the ears off them in there to reach our first final in 15 years, with Brian Cody as manager. But we lost to Young Irelands after a replay. It was their first title but they had some exceptional players, DJ Carey, Charlie Carter and Pat O'Neill being in and around their prime at that time.

DJ was the difference though as Gowran edged us out by two points. The two games are on YouTube and I watched them fairly recently. For one of DJ's goals, our goalkeeper Franny Cantwell never moved and was oblivious to the fact that it had hit the net as he looked around in bemusement. He suffered a lot of slagging for that since but nobody was laughing at the time, least of all my father. He was literally in tears coming out of Nowlan Park that day.

'We'll never win one,' he sobbed.

'You're just going to have to wait until I'm playing to win one,' I told him, as I often did for years afterwards.

##########

While there were players like Philly Larkin, Brian McEvoy and Peter Barry that I looked up to in a big way within the club, my hero growing up was undoubtedly DJ. He's who I wanted to be. He scored a sackful of goals but one that always stood out in my mind was his first against Galway in the 1997 All-Ireland quarter-final in Thurles, a day when he scored 2-8 and inspired a 10-point comeback. The goal was pure DJ; jet-heeled, leaving the Galway defence for dead before applying a typically lethal finish. I remember the same day, I fell into a supporters' flag, the bamboo going right into my eye. I had to get treated by the Order of Malta while the game went on.

I wore the numbers 12 and 14 quite frequently during my Kilkenny career, the two positions DJ occupied most often, but I concluded from an early age that, whatever I was, I wasn't going to be DJ Carey. Still, it doesn't stop you trying to recreate what he did when you're a youngster, and that goal was my *Phoenix From The Flames* moment more than any other.

While it's easy to recall flashy moments like that, there were other less celebrated aspects of his game that I tried to emulate. I was never going to match his pace, but his handpassing ability is something that was very much understated. It's something that I practised a lot and became particularly accurate at – with both hands. It's a very much underappreciated skill.

I loved how he used to feint to strike, only to delay it by killing the ball on his hurl again, leaving defenders floundering. Again, it's something that I would have tried myself as a young lad but wouldn't have had the neck to chance at adult level. You just wouldn't get away with it. Only DJ. I was awestruck when getting his autograph Meeting Kilkenny players then, and DJ especially, was like being introduced to a Premier League footballer.

Jamesie O'Connor was another player that I had a fondness for. Philly marked him in the 1997 All-Ireland semi-final and gave me the jersey that he swapped with him after the game. Well, I wore it for years afterwards, from when it hung over my 13-year-old frame up to just a couple of years ago when it was just absolutely worn out. Jamesie was such a lovely hurler.

It's difficult to compare players from different eras, the balls are different now and the pace of the game is a few strides faster, but there'll never be anyone quite like DJ again. Even Henry Shefflin, while he had qualities that DJ didn't have, he wouldn't have had his pace or even his skillset.

As it turned out, our careers intersected a little. His last year playing for Kilkenny was my first. It was surreal going in to share a dressing room with him in 2005. For the first couple of months I was a little bit in awe of him. It helped to drive me on though. If I was sharing a training field with him, I wanted to make a good impression and not let him think that I wasn't good enough to be there.

Our club careers overlapped too on a magical day in 2004 as James Stephens made it back to the county final with Gowran in opposition once again. It was a campaign in which I really turned a corner as a hurler and I have our manager, Adrian Finan, to thank for that. I'd been knocking around the senior team for a couple of years and then right from the start that year, he told me I was going in at centre-forward and he left me there. Moreover, I was on the frees, and I hit them well all year. It was a huge show of confidence in me. I'd never really played centre-forward coming through; I was mostly midfield or full-forward on underage teams. You couldn't say it was an obvious call on Adrian's part but him putting that faith in me gave me a right boost.

In the county final, we were well on our way when leading by eight points with eight minutes left before DJ emerged to put on an exhibition of striking that came within inches of condemning us to a defeat we might never have recovered from. Looking back, it was probably his last great exhibition on a big day. They got a point and then DJ drilled a free to the net, to which I replied with a pointed free. DJ buried another free and though Joe Murray hit back with a goal for us, DJ then converted a penalty. Two-point game.

Then Gowran got one last free from the 21 and DJ stepped up. Mercifully, it whistled just over Franny's crossbar. I think he said afterwards that it was the cleanest strike of the lot of them. Too clean, obviously. The referee played on from the puckout. I won possession from a ruck and didn't really know what to do with it. Betraying my greenness, I just threw it over my shoulder and hit it in towards the goal. Martin Carey came out and drove it down the field and the final whistle blew.

I clearly remember Peter Barry, who was captain, dropping

to his knees and taking off his helmet. He was crying his eyes out. I doubt he ever showed such emotion after any of his successes with Kilkenny. Having scored 0-11, 0-4 from play, I was elated but it was my first proper year of senior hurling; Peter had been through the ringer with the club for years and won nothing. I recall seeing Brian Cody wrapping his son, Donncha, our corner-back, in a hug out on the field. Even he couldn't get The Village over the line when he was the manager.

My father came running out onto the pitch in floods of tears once again but there the similarities with 1996 ended. Amid the bedlam on the field you couldn't have anything approaching a normal conversation but I reminded him later that night: 'Didn't I tell you we wouldn't win one until I was on the team?!' 'You were right,' he says, 'you were right!'

We went on to win the club All-Ireland after that and glided straight back into a county final the following year against an emerging Ballyhale Shamrocks side. They obviously had some big names, led by Henry Shefflin, and other players that had big futures ahead of them, but we certainly weren't going to be fearing them on the back of what we had done in the previous 12 months. There was a great unity in the club then. Everyone was just pushing the thing forward.

We won by three points and Henry had a bit of a nightmare. Perhaps the pressure of having to carry a young side like that got to him and he struck a lot of wides. He disappeared down the tunnel at the end of the match, which was bad form. Whatever about me, having only joined the county panel, he'd soldiered with Philly, Peter and Brian with Kilkenny for years.

The dynamic changed between us and Ballyhale after that, however. They came back and won four-in-a-row, beating us in the 2008 and '09 finals and a semi-final on top of that. I don't think, as a team, we really believed we could beat them. That utter conviction that you needed to take out a team of that quality just wasn't there.

We got back to another final against them in 2011, by which time we were managed by Niall Rigney, the former Laois hurler. He deserves enormous credit for what we achieved, particularly in how he picked us up off the floor after we drew with them the first day.

Ballyhale had a sort of air of invincibility in Kilkenny at that time and our failure to get over the line did little to diminish that, initially at least. I scored what looked to be the winning point on a filthy wet day only for Henry to convert a free in the fourth minute of injury time to ensure a replay. Niall addressed us in the dressing room straight after the game which lifted the mood a little but he recognised that it wasn't enough. We were up in the club later that evening and he pulled us all together into the back room. He spoke passionately, emphasising how we hadn't been beaten and that it was still there for us.

'What's all the doom and gloom about?' he snapped. 'We're going to play in a county final again next week, this is some opportunity for us.'

Our attitudes changed straight away. You still have to go out and prepare for the game and perform to win it, but without that intervention we most certainly would not have won it. Niall's ability to lift us was all the more remarkable for the fact that he later told me that he broke down in tears in the car alongside his wife after the game. On the back of that, he quickly convinced himself that it wasn't gone and then he transmitted that to us.

For me personally, the replay was just one of those days where everything clicked. From 12 shots, I scored 1-11. Eddie Brennan later spoke about my display in the context of what he had seen DJ do over the years for club and county and described it as 'the greatest individual hurling exhibition I ever saw', which meant a hell of a lot coming from him. DJ was such an idol for me growing up and for Eddie, arguably Kilkenny's next best goalscorer after him, to put my display above any of his was a phenomenal compliment.

In the lead-up to the drawn game, knowing I'd be playing centre-forward, I was stressing to myself how I'd cover all of that area, out on the wings and into midfield on puckouts so that if anything breaks, I'm on to it. But the weather was atrocious. The game just didn't lend itself to doing that as you'd want to, so bad were the conditions. I made the same vow ahead of the replay and I covered every blade of grass, picking up breaks, taking and making scores. Looking back at the match, there were times when I had three or four Ballyhale lads around me and I'd wonder how I got the ball away but I just shoved them out of the way. Nothing was going to stop me this day.

Coming towards half-time I chased back one of their players well into our half and after he lost possession, I picked it up and ran all the way up the field with Cha Fitzpatrick giving chase.

He eventually tripped me at around their 65. I didn't feel like I needed any respite, I just jumped straight up and put the free over the bar. I did a lot of that sort of thing on that particular day.

We didn't play that well as a team in the first half and were four points down when I got a goal. A ball broke for me from a ruck around the 21. There were six Shamrocks players in the vicinity but I found a way through and finished to the corner of the net. I scored a free after that and we were level at half-time. Eamonn Walsh had been marking me and then Michael Fennelly was switched to centre-back, as Walsh went centre-forward on Jackie. The game was now being played on our terms.

We naturally identified TJ Reid as a huge threat and detailed Eamonn Sheehy to man-mark him. Well, if TJ had to go for a piss that day, Eamonn would have been in the jacks beside him. Niall Rigney texted me a few months later when watching the video of the game noting how TJ ran over the ball at one stage and Eamonn ran over it with him. I often chided TJ about it afterwards. 'Eamonn Sheehy is coming for you!' 'Oh keep that c**t away from me, I don't want to see him ever again!' It was one of those days where we were just on the right side of manic. We pulled away to win by eight points in the end and it probably could have been more.

It was mayhem up in the clubhouse afterwards. It was a sweet victory because, six years after we'd won an All-Ireland, it was widely assumed that we just didn't have a performance like that in us anymore. There were lads who'd rarely get carried away that were in the horrors. Tracey Millea and I even did a duet of 'Don't Stop Believing' at one stage.

The trouble was, we had to play Oulart-The Ballagh in the Leinster quarter-final the following Sunday. Jackie got a straight red card in the second half of the replay and was suspended. They built a lead on us but we were drawing them back when we ran out of time. Another few minutes and we might have had them. No doubt the proximity of the county final replay didn't help and it would be something of a regret that the celebrations bled into our preparation for Oulart but it wouldn't be an overbearing one either because county finals are so bloody hard to win and you have to celebrate them when you do.

There's nothing quite like winning, or losing, with your club on county final day.

##########

Wednesday, October 31, 2018

Hallowe'en night in Derry. Work have put me and a colleague, Maurice Quinlan, up for the night after we had done a bit of networking up here. There's a huge festival and we rounded off a productive trip with a few pints of this new Rockshore stuff, which I'm warming to. I'm certainly warming to my new job too and am well settled. Yesterday I got my first sale over the line, a client in Mayo, having gone down to meet him previously with one of our business development managers. That got a cheer in the office and an email from Tom Butler. 'The Cats are back!' he wrote.

Maurice is more experienced than I am so the idea of us going together was so I could observe him in meetings and how he operates. Initially, when I started, much of my correspondence was over email, as it allows you to converse with clients without your lack of experience being exposed. Then I started getting on the phone a bit more and meeting clients face to face is the next logical progression.

Again, there are times when the hurling background can be used to my advantage, without abusing it. The Donnelly Group in Tyrone is one company that we were looking to do business with. I noticed that Philip Jordan, the former Tyrone footballer, works for them and fired him off an email recently. Never met him before but felt that our similar backgrounds would help me make inroads with him quicker than someone else might, and so it proved. I've to chat to him again in a few weeks.

I love the hours, Monday-Friday, weekends off, the office 10 minutes from my house. I intend to play club hurling for another couple of years but, had I stayed doing shift work in Dublin, I would have packed it in after this year.

3

NOVEMBER

*'How would you feel about coming
into the Kilkenny panel?'*
'Jesus, I'd be delighted with that!'

Saturday, November 3, 2018

Paul Murphy got in touch a few weeks ago wondering would I take part in a benefit match for Amanda Stapleton, sister of Paddy, who played at corner-back for Tipperary for a number of years. It would be a Tipperary-Kilkenny game, largely featuring players from the 2009-11 All-Ireland finals.

Sadly, Amanda has an inoperable brain tumour so her family are desperately trying to raise funds to meet costs for treatment and make life that little bit easier for her. It doesn't take me long to say yes to something like that, especially for Paddy. He was always a likeable chap and there was never any bullshit about him, on or off the field. It was all about the ball when he was marking you, no digging or mouthing.

Paul set up a WhatsApp group and there was a big turnout from our side as we travelled down to Borrisoleigh today. We got a bus and the craic was good.

'I'm going to drop a ball at some lad's feet and let fly,' I declared on the way down to roars of laughter.

The Liam MacCarthy Cup may not have been on offer to the winner but, naturally enough, the game was fairly competitive. It wasn't played at the same pace as the club games I've been involved in in the last few weeks but it zipped along all the same. I would have feared that the game was starting to get away from me a little at times this year but I felt good tonight and hit 1-3.

The edge was still there between the two teams. JJ Delaney challenged Seamus Callanan at one stage as he was trying to rise the ball and was slapping him fairly relentlessly with both hands. I said to JJ at half-time, 'Do you not like Callanan or what's the story?!'

'Ah he doesn't fucking like me either!' JJ replied.

DJ Carey was managing us and Liam Sheedy reprised his role with Tipperary. I was burning oil with 20 minutes to go, my ankles and knees were creaking. I looked over for someone to come in for me and there was Henry Shefflin, Jackie Tyrrell, Michael Kavanagh and JJ on the line, but none of them wanted to go back on.

Henry has stopped hurling completely now but he still looked sharp enough in the first half, albeit he was like a mummy going around the place, so heavily bandaged was his knee! We scored a goal in the first half that made me feel nostalgic. Henry got a ball around the 45 on the left wing and he picked out a pass to me to make it a two-on-one. That was something we always tried to do over the years, play a ball to create an overlap like that and no better man than Henry to find you, even as he's closing in on 40 years of age. I laid it off to Aidan Fogarty and he buried it.

We were maybe seven or eight points down with a few minutes to go and our belligerence kicked in to ensure we got a draw. Nobody made any declarations about what we wanted to get out of the game but we certainly wouldn't have wanted to lose it. In truth, these type of games can often be a pain in the arse but this one was competitive and enjoyable to be involved in. The whole set-up was fantastic. There was a marquee and we had a few drinks afterwards.

It was brilliant being back among the lads again and catching up, poring over old times. Whatever the perception of us may be, we always had brilliant craic together over the years. We couldn't have been as successful as we were if we hadn't.

I remember on one All Star trip to San Francisco, a group of us, mostly Kilkenny lads, went to a 49ers game and we took in the tailgating outside the stadium beforehand. We effectively gatecrashed a bunch of Americans, who started giving us all sorts of food. Sure enough, we ran out of drink, despite bringing enough to intoxicate an army, so a few of us marched back to the nearest store for more.

We got a load of cans and two big bottles of vodka, carried by Richie Power and Tommy Walsh.

On the way back we were crossing a bridge and Tommy, completely scuttered, announced: 'We've too much drink here lads, we've too much drink!'

Next thing he just threw his bottle of vodka down into the water below as Richie screeched: 'Don't! Don't!' I'm not exaggerating when I say that Richie wore the look of a man who had just been bereaved.

'What did you do Tommy?!'

'Oh we had too much drink lads, we had too much drink…' Tommy kept saying as we made our way back up.

Sure enough, supplies began to run low again. 'I fucking told ya,' says Power, as the last of the vodka was drained. Tommy was feeling sheepish at this stage. Then he disappeared.

'Where's Tommy?' This certainly wasn't unusual. He had a habit, when he was pissed, of just slipping away without a word and off home to bed. We just presumed this was Tommy's latest Irish goodbye. 'I'd say he's gone, he's fucked.'

Next thing he reappeared carrying two bottles of vodka. 'Hey, hey!' he cried, holding them up. Jesus, it was so funny. But at least Richie was happy again.

I didn't get to see Amanda before we left Borrisoleigh but a few of the lads said she was there for a while. We don't have an especially good or bad relationship with the Tipperary players from that era.

I guess I'd speak for a lot of the Kilkenny lads by saying that I could take them or leave them. But that's all irrelevant in the greater scheme of things when you look at what that family is going through now. You wouldn't wish that on anybody.

They're clearly genuine people and that's why they got such a great turnout tonight.

##########

Monday, November 19, 2018

I was supposed to meet John McGuinness, Fianna Fáil TD for Carlow-Kilkenny this evening, to further tease out the possibility of my running for the party in the 2019 local elections. But I called Joe Malone this afternoon and called it off. There was no point wasting their time. I have no intention of running. I told Joe that and he was sound about it.

I suppose it's nice to be thought of and asked to put your name forward for something like that and there was the initial frisson of excitement when I was. It's easy to get a little carried away when you think about it at first. I didn't have a particular moment of clarity about it as such, but the more I mulled over it, the more I concluded that it just wasn't for me.

The canvassing involved would be quite extensive as the electoral area is rather big. If I was going to do it, I wouldn't do it half-arsed. I'd have to do all the canvassing that was required and then some. I didn't want to have a situation where I didn't give it my all and then be left wondering what might have been had I lost out by a few votes. I'd have to be out several nights a week in the months leading up to the election. Was I prepared to do that? Ultimately, no. And all of that would be required just to give yourself a chance of being elected. If you were elected then, it's another huge drain on your time and energy.

I'm still playing club hurling and hope to for another couple of years yet. I'm managing the club's under-19 team and enjoying it. That's something I don't want to push to the side either. I've just started a new job and didn't want a situation where I'd be looking for time off in the run-up to the election. Then there's my family life, which is quite hectic and with Anne after carrying the can for long enough when I was playing for Kilkenny, it wouldn't be fair to ask her to do so again. As it is, we don't spend enough time together as a family and this is two years after I retired from inter-county hurling. If I was more established in the job, if the kids were a bit older, if I wasn't still hurling, perhaps I would have thought longer and harder and come to a different conclusion. And maybe it's something I'll revisit in the future.

And maybe not. Some of the stuff that goes with being a politician is just completely anathema to me. I'm the worst in the world for going to funerals of people that I know. I'm hardly going to start going to those for people that I don't.

##########

In other news, Séamas 'Cheddar' Plunkett is to be the next James Stephens senior hurling manager. It was quite an exhaustive process to find someone after Niall Tyrrell stepped down.

In the club, there's a hurling committee put in place at the end of the year to oversee the appointment of management teams through all the grades and I agreed to sit on it. Obviously it's important to get the right people in place for every team but the senior hurlers are the club's flagship team and I wanted to get involved to avoid a situation where the committee just gave it to someone for the sake of giving it to someone.

There were elements of the committee that favoured an inside appointment but I just wanted the best man we could get, wherever he was from. The most high profile and alluring candidate was Derek McGrath and, for a while, I thought we had him. We haven't tended to go for big-name appointments in our club and we haven't exactly been tearing it up over the last few years so, for me, it was certainly worth considering.

Obviously McGrath adopted a defensive template when in charge of Waterford but that didn't worry me. If he was to take charge of us, once he saw what was available to him, I'd be surprised if he concluded that that would be the way to go. I felt that the sweeper system that he employed with Waterford was specific to where they were, having suffered some heavy beatings in the first year that he was with them.

Any doubts I had about him were more centred on his personality: would he be too nice? I've long felt that we're mentally weak and we tend to respond better to managers dogging us rather than being our best friend. Now, maybe Derek McGrath can do that, I don't know. I won't be finding out any time soon anyway.

Murty Leahy, one of the lads who was on the committee, is involved in greyhounds along with some people from Portlaw who know McGrath. So he rang him and sounded him out. Murty wasn't met with a stone wall but McGrath hemmed and hawed a lot about it. 'I'm going to get Eoin Larkin to ring you,' Murty told him. 'Don't get him to ring me because he'll change my mind!' came the reply. I called Derek but he was on holiday in Spain and he texted me to say he'd ring me back the next morning, which he did.

I had never spoken to him before but I had already formed a good impression. When he'd come into our dressing room after we played Waterford, there seemed to be a great sincerity about him in how he spoke. I've heard enough managers in that scenario that are absolutely full of shit to know the difference.

Anyway, we had a great chat. It was really positive and he made it clear that he was delighted to be offered such a role with us. I told him how I admired the unity that he brought to the Waterford players, something I thought we were badly lacking as, too often, we played as individuals. He told me to press ahead with drawing up a shortlist while he mulled things over but he did say, 'Look, I'll come up and talk to ye one way or the other.'

Ultimately, he didn't do that, which was a little disappointing. I was in contact with him through text subsequently and eventually he sent me a text saying that he needed another few months to recharge the batteries and that he had committed to a summer holiday with his family next year, the first opportunity they'd had to do that in a number of years.

We made contact with Willie Maher from Tipperary too but he wasn't available. A few weeks later he was announced as Cuala's new manager. There was contact with one or two others and I tried Niall Rigney also but he had had enough of management, per se. He just wanted to coach and if we could get someone in the club who would look after the more cumbersome aspects of the role, he'd be happy to come and talk to us but there was no one really suited to that.

At one stage, there seemed to be a groundswell of support for Philly Larkin and word was out that he was keen but eventually the word came back was that he had been interested but, having thought it through, didn't have the time.

Then there was the outgoing management team, which

certainly hadn't been jettisoned en masse on the back of Niall Tyrrell standing down as while we didn't get to where we wanted this year, it didn't mean that they got everything wrong. Séamus Dwyer, the coach, was certainly someone who had impressed me greatly. From Ballinakill, he's a teacher in Kilkenny CBS and that's how Niall had got him involved. Like Niall Rigney, he'd rather be a coach than a manager but he had worked with Cheddar in Laois and we thought they might make a good team with us. So we asked Séamus to get in touch with him.

He turned out to be the kingmaker. Séamus knew that we needed an injection of something and Cheddar's enthusiasm might just be it. He agreed to take the job though won't be coming on board full-time until June 1 as he has other things going on in the meantime. That might appear to be a little unsatisfactory but it doesn't bother me in the slightest. We're only going to have a few league games in April and then we won't be playing again until August. Anyway, Séamus tells me that he's been on the phone to him every day already. I expect we'll be seeing a lot of Cheddar before June 1.

The whole experience of sitting on the committee was an eye-opening one. I've long felt that we've taken our eye off the ball in the club, particularly since we developed new grounds on the Kells Road. It became all about the Kells Road.

Now there are plans to put a kitchen in up there that will cost a fortune yet, by all accounts, it will only be used a few times a year. And the first thing I heard as soon as I joined the committee was 'we don't have the money, lads'. Where are your priorities? The senior hurling team is the most important entity in the club and county final day is what we should always be building towards in any given year but, in my opinion, some people have lost sight of that.

Players generally separate themselves completely from what goes on in the administrative side of things and are often the first to give out about decisions that are taken. Having moved over to the other side, I have a much greater understanding of how tough and wearisome it can be. We all scratch our heads at some decisions that are made by GAA committees at club, county, provincial and national level and wonder how the hell did they arrive at them. After this experience, I'd conclude that, quite often, it just comes down to getting things done rather than doing things right.

Some of the meetings would go on and on and you'd lose the will to contribute for fear of dragging things out any further. One night I was a broken man listening to it all and was happy to let the meeting conclude despite it having veered in what I believed was an unsatisfactory direction. It was only when I thought about it the next day that I said, 'No, this can't happen' and lifted the phone. But it's very easy to fall into the trap of going with the flow just for the sake of getting the hell out of there. It's important to take a step back and ask *is this the right decision or is it just a decision to get it done and dusted?* A couple of others on the committee were of a similar outlook to me and we felt there was a danger of the job just being pitched at someone in the club. 'Here, will you do that?'

I'm 35 next year. My club career is rapidly drawing to a close. I can't afford an *ah-sure-it'll-do* appointment at this stage. More importantly, the team can't. Hopefully Cheddar's the man.

##########

Sunday, November 25, 2018

Kilkenny Under-19 'A' hurling final:
O'Loughlin Gaels 2-13 James Stephens 1-14.

My own managerial career took flight this year and my first assignment ended in heartbreaking circumstances today. The group of players that I took charge of haven't had much in the way of success, a minor football title at the start of this year being the first championship that they had won together. O'Loughlins have been their nemesis right up along.

Last year they beat us in the minor final, though I wasn't involved. From talking to some who were, there was a feeling that we didn't give ourselves the best chance of winning the game having packed the defence with our better players in a bid to contain them. I was determined that we wouldn't go that route this year.

I worked quite hard to infuse them with the belief that they were good enough to take O'Loughlins on and beat them, particularly in the fortnight between the semi-final and the final. 'We have total confidence in ye,' I told them, 'we're not man-marking anyone, we don't care who's playing for them or who isn't playing, we just want ye to go at them and show them who's boss.' There would have been numerous follow-ups on that theme on our WhatsApp group as well. We had them in for a chat for about 20 minutes last night and they appeared to be very focused.

In the end, we didn't quite get there today. We didn't play well in the first half and still only went in two points down having conceded a bad goal. We did much better in the second half but gave away another sloppy goal and had one disallowed ourselves. We were in the ascendency come the end and had it gone on for another few minutes, we might have got them but it was the first half display that rankled the most. Had we hurled just a little bit better in the opening half hour we probably would have won it. It's a different kind of disappointment to the senior team going out last month; this time I'm devastated for the players after the effort they put in.

But you can't weight success solely on whether you pick up the trophy at the end of the year. There were a few players on the team today that would have been miles off it 12 months ago. There's great satisfaction in that and the junior management deserve credit for giving them game time during the year, it helped develop them no end. Most credit goes to those players themselves, however. They were supremely dedicated all year and a manager's dream - you knew when you called training that they were always going to be there. The upshot of all that is we now have a bigger panel to pick from going forward.

I'm conscious of how important these years are for young players' development given my own experiences, albeit I was a bit younger than the current under-19 group are now when I had what I would say was the turning point in my underage career. When I was under-14, I was drafted onto the under-16 team as a goalkeeper, a role that I continued with the club's minor team when I was still under-16. I was generally midfield when playing in my own age group but I liked playing in goals and it was good for my confidence to be hurling with an older age group. That evaporated, however, when we played Ballyhale in the minor league final in what would have been Jackie Tyrrell's last year as a minor in 2000. We were in front by a couple of points when a long ball came in and trickled off my fingers and into the net. Then the same thing happened a few minutes later. Two desperately soft goals. It cost us the match and it was devastating for me.

It probably didn't help that the lads I was playing with weren't really my friends as such, given that they were a couple of years older. I remember my father trying to talk to me about it and I just shrugged it off. 'Yeah, I'm grand,' I lied. But I decided on the back of it that I wasn't going to play in goals anymore. Looking back, it was probably a bit abrupt given that I'd been doing it for a couple of years at that stage with no major mishaps. Jackie's father, Dermot, was manager of the minor team and I went to him and his selector, Liam O'Connor, and told them that I wanted to come out of goals. 'Well, you won't be guaranteed your place out the field,' I was informed. 'That's fair enough, I'll fight for it,' I insisted.

We had a couple of games after that in which I was brought on without doing a whole lot. Then, as the county semi-final, also against Ballyhale, approached, I was starting to find some form. We were behind when I was introduced and I helped to turn the game in our favour, setting up a couple of goals. We still lost but it did a huge amount for my confidence. It carried me into the following year, my first as a minor hurler only, and though we didn't have a great team, I emerged as one of the main players.

The experience of the year before after coming out of goals gave me the confidence to go and dominate games against lads of my own age. I'd been going through a little bit of a phase where I could take or leave hurling around then but I really drove on from there. I've seen similar progress in a few of the under-19s this year.

I was a selector with the club's under-21s a few years back but it's a different story when you have the bainisteoir's bib on your back. I had Davy Tyrrell, Niall's brother, and Tomás O'Dowd with me as selectors. They were a great aid and I learned a lot from them. We complemented each other well. I found at times that I got too engrossed in games but they were able to give me a different perspective which, when I stood back a bit, I was able to see.

On the whole, I think we covered all bases fairly well. We had Niall Tyrrell and Séamus Dwyer above in the stand keeping an eye on things for us and I asked them, along with others in the club, afterwards if there was anything we could or should have done on the line. They all said that we did as much as we could and there's comfort in that. I haven't run into Brian Cody just yet though!

In terms of where my managerial career goes, I don't really have any grand long-term ambitions. I'm not necessarily building towards the Kilkenny job though I'd like to think I'd get a shot with The Village senior team at some stage. If I don't, it won't be the end of the world either. Once I stop playing I'll have more time to put into the coaching side of it but I wouldn't see myself becoming one of these super coaches with drills coming out of my ears. I'm not a fan of that sort of thing; there's too much of it these days.

Would you define Brian Cody as a coach? No, I wouldn't think so. In this day and age, you probably need to differentiate between being a coach or a manager; I'd see myself as someone who would be more inclined towards management but wouldn't cut myself off from the coaching side of things either.

I enjoyed the experience with the under-19s this year and I'll take it on again next year. It wasn't too hard to get that through the hurling committee!

##########

I can clearly remember Brian Cody, when he was my teacher in sixth class, calling me up to his desk one day. He didn't carry quite the reputation that he does now but he was manager of The Village senior team at the time and had captained Kilkenny to an All-Ireland. That was enough to give him prominence in my world. So when he showed me the team that he had picked for an upcoming match with the school with 'C' written beside my name, I was absolutely chuffed.

'What do you think of that?' he asked.

'Oh, I'm delighted with that,' I replied.

As captain, it was my job to go around to the other lads and tell them the team and the arrangements for the game. It gave me a bit of status and confidence and it was probably the first time that someone had shown that sort of faith in me as a hurler.

##########

The last Sunday in November in 2004, James Stephens were crowned Leinster club champions after surfing the momentum from our first county title in 23 years. My form had been pretty seamless from the Kilkenny campaign; I hit

3-18 in our games against Kilmessan, Oulart-The Ballagh and UCD. Oulart still had Liam Dunne and Martin Storey, right at the fag end of their careers. Storey was 40 and playing what was supposed to be his last game but he still clipped three points. Dunne was centre-back and marking me, something which was on my mind coming into it as his reputation preceded him at the time but it passed off without incident. I was happy enough to get 1-4 from play in a game we won by five points after struggling for a lot of the first half.

UCD had a stellar line-up in the final with the likes of Brian Hogan, Brian Barry, Stephen Lucey, Brendan Murphy and Redmond Barry in their ranks. After we ran up a 10-point first half lead, they came storming back and we were relieved to hang on for a one-point victory in the end. The momentum we had was huge at this stage. After the county final, we felt that no one could get in our way and that confidence really stood to us against seasoned opposition in Leinster.

Naturally, I was feeling good about myself as I got dressed afterwards in the O'Moore Park dressing room. I was the last one left, or so I thought until Brian Cody appeared beside me. Since he had taught me in school, my dealings with him had been fairly minimal. He was now a three-time All-Ireland winning manager with an ever-expanding reputation.

'Great win today,' he opened.

'Yeah, great win, we got over the line in the end,' I replied.

'How would you feel about coming into the Kilkenny panel?'

'Jesus, I'd be delighted with that!'

'Well, you'll be coming in after March, with the help of God.'

'With the help of God, yeah.'

And that was pretty much it. It was a surreal way for it to happen. Brian is obviously a Village man and his son, Donncha, was on the team at the time so it was natural enough that he would be hanging around the dressing room after a game like that. Most lads would tend to get a phone call but it was a great feeling and a moment I'll never forget.

I still had a long way to go as a hurler but my game had improved more in the couple of months leading up to that Leinster club final than it ever did before or since. That September I couldn't command a starting place on the Kilkenny under-21 team and, in all fairness, I couldn't really have any great complaints. I still had another year to go at that age group, Kilkenny had won the All-Ireland the year before and I would have needed to shoot the lights out to leapfrog lads who were much more established. I was an impact sub as we won the All-Ireland again, beating Tipperary by 12 points in the final so you couldn't say that the team management, led by Martin Fogarty, got it wrong and I felt they gave me a much fairer hearing that I had got at minor level a couple of years earlier.

But I definitely bloomed once I got back in with the club and my confidence took off, especially after the county final. Despite all that, I didn't see a Kilkenny call-up as an inevitability or anything like it and, in truth, hadn't even thought about it. That made it all the sweeter when it happened and I was buzzing walking out of O'Moore Park that day, eagerly looking forward to telling my father, who was always the first one to hear about developments like this.

It capped off what had been a brilliant couple of months. I couldn't have dreamed what was to follow on the back of it.

4
—

DECEMBER

*'I always wanted them to get back together and,
in my youthful innocence, believed it was only a
matter of time before they would'*

Sunday, December 2, 2018

I t's two years today since I ceased to be a Kilkenny hurler. In the end, I made the decision rather quickly. It just hit me right between the eyes. 'I'm not going to be able to do this.' And then I lifted the phone to set various things in motion that would officially bring my inter-county career to an end. I had already gone back training with the team, for maybe five sessions, and was trying to work out a way that would allow me to play on into 2017 but it was never going to be workable. The catalyst for it all was my decision to leave the army and take up a job in Pfizer, based in Saggart on the west side of Dublin.

My mother has a mobile home in Tramore and we'd go down there a bit. On one occasion Anne and I were down with James Holden, one of my friends, and his wife Carol, and we got chatting about his job in Pfizer. He mentioned the sort of money he was on and it dwarfed what I was getting.

Money had always been a concern as long as I had been in the army as we earned a pittance though, at the same time, I had never put serious thought into leaving. But when James told me all about the salary and benefits that he had in Pfizer, it really got me thinking. There were jobs available up there and after a couple of weeks I decided to apply for the role of process technician.

I had no experience in that area but Pfizer are one of the few pharmaceutical companies who will give people who haven't worked in the field before a shot. I went through all the various channels and had an interview where I was quizzed on how I'd deal with different situations based on my time in the army. Eventually I was offered the job and I accepted it.

The vast increase in salary was a big factor but so too was the time off. I was only required to work 14 days a month, albeit they were all 12-hour shifts, day and night, starting at 6.45am or 6.45pm.

Straight away, that was going to impact on training one way or the other, while the shifts also stretched across weekends and so would impact on availability for matches in a big way. I'd have to obliterate my annual leave and even that probably wouldn't be enough either. I was going to be working every second weekend anyway.

I spoke to Brian Cody about it and then Michael Dempsey, to see would there be a way to get around it training-wise given that Mick designs the sessions in winter. 'Could you not tell them you'll take it in a year's time and stay in the army for another year?' Brian asked me. It wasn't something that I wanted to do, though. I'd had 12 years of inter-county hurling and concluded that I had enough. I just didn't want any more of it. It had been a difficult year on top of that for various reasons, which made it that bit easier to let go.

Another factor was the possibility of being a sub. Brian had said to me, 'I don't know if you're going to be playing next year or whether you'll be coming on or starting or whether you'll last 70 minutes. Only you can decide that.'

I had always said that I'd keep going with Kilkenny once I felt I had something to offer, even if that meant not playing and passing on my experience to the younger lads. But then once the possibility of that happening started to become more apparent, it was hard to stomach. I was satisfied that I had won so much and had a good career. I wanted to live my life again. I was 32, which wasn't especially old, but it was getting more difficult for my body to recover and I wanted to give a couple of good years to the club before I was completely wrecked.

Still, I mulled over it for a few weeks. Then I was in my mother's house one Thursday when it just hit me. And that was it. Decision made.

I called Brian within an hour and told him. 'Yeah look, it's probably not going to work if you're taking the job,' he said. 'You've had a great career and done some great things. You'll see what's thought of you once you announce it.' I was still in my mother's house and I borrowed my sister's laptop and started to write my retirement statement:

After due consideration I have decided that now is the right time for me to announce my inter-county retirement. I have enjoyed 12 of the best years of my life with success I could only have dreamed of. It was always my dream from a young age to play, captain and win an All-Ireland with Kilkenny and I'm proud and happy to say I lived my dream. I am content to walk away now knowing I gave everything I could for myself but also the team every time I walked out on the training pitch or pulled on a Kilkenny jersey and left no stone unturned in the pursuit of perfection, although I never got close. I've played with and against some of the best players of all time and had the privilege of working with the best manager of all time for those years...

It ran on to more than 500 words. I called Ned Quinn, the county chairman, and emailed it to him. Séamus Reade, the PRO, then issued it to the local and national media the following morning. There were a few loose ends to tie up before it went public. I called to my father the night before and I think he was a bit shocked; he didn't say too much but he did say, 'I would have been happy with you winning one All-Ireland but now you have eight.' I got a bit emotional and shed a few tears. The finality of it was hitting me.

It was the end of an era for my wider family, I suppose, as they would have had a lot of great years going along to Kilkenny matches that I was playing in. But I don't think they were too cut up about it. My mother would hardly sit in the seat at a match anyway. She'd be out the back smoking with Mary Tyrrell, Jackie's mother, too nervous to watch. 'I'm not giving you a ticket,' I used to tell her, 'it's a waste.' 'Oh I have to be there, I have to be there.'

My own family was grand about it. Anne was probably delighted privately! The kids just shrugged and didn't say much. Holly would often come home and say, 'My friend was going on to me today, she didn't realise Eoin Larkin was my father, so embarrassing, like.' So at least that stigma was being removed from their lives!

These days, a big part of retiring revolves around the team WhatsApp group. I sent a message to it, along with Mick Dempsey, Derek Lyng and James McGarry, informing them that a statement would be coming out shortly on my retirement. I said I hoped that I had left the jersey in a better place than where I found it. That was hard. Once I sent the message I immediately went to leave the group. My thumb hovered over the exit button and I hesitated before finally pressing it.

Pádraig Walsh was soon on to me. I had been back doing the running with the squad in Dunmore ahead of the 2017 season and he texted, 'I thought we had ya for another year when you came back training!' He added some nice sentiment on what it was like to play with me and complimented me on my service to Kilkenny. I had found the running difficult but, the thing is, if I'd stayed in the army I would almost certainly have kept going for another year.

Brian was right in what he said – my phone was hopping for the next few days and I got lots of nice messages. One from Ken McGrath stood out in particular. He congratulated me on my career and said I had been as important to Kilkenny as JJ or Henry.

Jackie had only announced his retirement a couple of weeks before and I was a little anxious that people would link the two but it had nothing to do with my decision, even if he was the last of the players that I was particularly friendly with to depart. There had been a couple of years where we suffered a spate of retirements in a short space of time, 2014 in particular with JJ, Tommy, David Herity, Brian Hogan and Aidan Fogarty all going before Henry followed them after the club campaign the following March. As the departures mounted up, Conor Fogarty chimed in at one stage on the WhatsApp group, 'Ah Jaysus lads, not another one, we won't have a team next year!'

Generally when someone retires, there's a bit of banter on the group for 10 minutes or so; you might get a few tearful emojis and tributes and then that's it. Everyone moves on, which is how it should be.

You'd think you'd miss all these big characters in the dressing room when training resumes but I never really found it to be like that. You wouldn't have too much talking and geeing up at that stage of the year anyway. When the time for that would come around later in the year, all the retirees are gone a good few months at that stage and the dressing room has evolved without them. You had until May or June to get that dynamic right before leaders and talkers start to emerge. Still, you might be out on a session after a game and say, 'Jaysus, you'd miss Tommy out on the beer, wouldn't ya?' But that would be it. With regard to training, you just got on with it.

A few months after we had retired, there was a night in the club for Jackie and me. Michael Duignan did MC and Davy Fitzgerald and John Mullane came along too and spoke, along with a host of former teammates. A big crowd turned out and we each got Aer Lingus vouchers for €500 and DID, the club sponsors, gave us both a smart watch.

I found the move to being a former Kilkenny hurler pretty frictionless to be honest. There was a relief, if anything, that I wasn't chasing my tail so much. I felt that I could sit back and relax. I cut myself off from it and certainly couldn't claim to have been a fanatical supporter during the early stages of retirement. Not that that was a conscious decision either. It's just that, while I kept tabs on how they were progressing, I didn't go to any championship games the year after I retired.

I remember watching the Waterford match, which they lost after extra time, down in Tramore having taken another visit down to my mother's mobile home. I just wanted to go and watch a match in comfort without having the hassle that goes with getting to a game and getting home.

The first Kilkenny championship game I attended since retiring was the Wexford game in Nowlan Park a year and a half after I'd departed and I can't say it felt weird. It was a bit of craic actually because I was on the terrace behind the goal with a few lads. I went down to the Limerick game in Thurles then a few weeks later. Maybe I'll go to more matches in the future. But not them all. There are other priorities now.

############

December saw both the beginning and the end of my time in the army too, 12 years apart. Having left school after my Junior Cert in 2000, I worked that summer in a cash and carry and then my father was getting a job done on his kitchen by Philly

Houlihan when he asked him would there be any apprenticeships going for a young lad like me. He took me on for more than three years as a cabinet-maker. Philly eventually had to let me go because the numbers weren't stacking up with the amount of staff he had and I then had a spell with the late Duxie Walsh, the famous handballer, before moving on to Paul Dowling in Muckalee. I enjoyed the work and the independence that it brought after all the torrid years I had in school.

I hadn't yet finished my apprenticeship when I decided to apply for the army. I had been let go from a couple of different jobs with the cabinet-making and wanted something steady and reliable where I knew my wages would be in the bank every week. My mother's husband, Paddy, was a soldier and I used to envy how on some Monday mornings he didn't have to be in the barracks when I'd be heading out the door to work with a banging hangover. I had wanted to join when I first left school but my father put his foot down on that one, at least partially because of the fact that Paddy was in it and they weren't on good terms at the time.

There were other family connections too. My aunt, Lorraine Donovan, is in the army and so too had my late aunt Anna Norris's husband John, who also died some years ago. I had a couple of cousins in it too. I'd seen them all go overseas and it was appealing. So I applied, did the interview, the medical and the fitness test and was accepted. There were two platoons at the time, one went to Limerick and the other to Kilkenny, where I started my training in the James Stephens Barracks as a recruit on December 15, 2004. Joining as a cadet wasn't an option for me as I didn't have my Leaving Cert at the time.

The recruit training lasted five months which made you a two star private and then you're required to do another 10 weeks' two to three star course. The training was tough, both physically and mentally. Most people's impression of it would be drawn from films like Full Metal Jacket and, while you wouldn't have someone like R Lee Ermey's Gunnery Sergeant Hartman thundering around the place or fellas spitting in your face or beating you with bars of soap, it is quite similar. The challenge is not to laugh while they're roaring at you that 'the rooms are so dirty up there, even the rats are wearing overalls'.

You live in the barracks during training and you can't leave unless you have a pass signed by an officer. It was generally Monday to Friday but sometimes they'd keep you in at the weekend. Just to melt your head.

We'd generally rise at 7am for breakfast at 7.30am and while back then you could get a fry, they've moved towards a more healthy meal to start the day now. As I recall, the money was a bit over €200 a week and you'd have €40 taken out for your meals. After breakfast we'd have an inspection of the uniforms and would don the number ones for that. We'd all tend to keep one good uniform specifically for this exercise and it would have to be perfectly ironed with the boots sparkling. Everything about you could be pristine but they'd still throw you off the parade, just because. A bit of dust on your beret or something anal like that. The punishment could range from press-ups to a 10-page essay on something obscure like, say, the inside of a golf ball.

After lunch we'd invariably have weapons training. We could also have a presentation on military history and there'd be plenty of physical work too, like a 10km run. There'd be route marches, hill walks, military circuits, map reading and navigation exercises. I found the whole thing tough going, particularly from a physical point of view, while it would really test you mentally too. I know now that no matter how perfect our uniforms were on inspection, if they had made their minds up that they were going to pick on you, that was it. They just wanted to see how you'd react under pressure.

Not everyone could take it. There was one chap from Cork who wasn't cut out for it at all. The fact that he came up to Kilkenny on a moped was an early indicator. When we were on the range, we had to make sure the barrel of the rifle was clear and we'd dust it out, but one day he left a big lump of cloth wedged in it. If he had to fire a round out of that, anything could have happened.

I remember the look of incredulity on the sergeant's face as he stared at him. 'Are you fucking stupid or what?' They were bawling at him day after day and, unsurprisingly, he didn't last. Some of the stuff that they'd roar would be over the top but you have to put it into context too. It didn't bother me at all but some people would take it to heart. There were 40 in the group with about seven or eight dropouts over the five months. Some lads concluded after a couple of weeks that it just wasn't for them. Others couldn't hack it physically or mentally and the corporals or platoon lieutenant or sergeant would just crack them.

One of the corporals that trained me was Stephen Grehan, the Kilkenny hurler. It used to be great when we had him as he was a good laugh but we'd still get the work done. He was just one of the lads that was more chilled out about it. At the time of my training, James Stephens were on a run to the All-Ireland club title and I used to get a pass in the evening to go training. If we were being kept in at the weekend, I'd get out too as required for the hurling. They were fairly accommodating that way in fairness. When we won the All-Ireland club final, the match fell on a Thursday so they left me off on the Wednesday night until the following Sunday evening.

By the end of my five months, I was in the Kilkenny senior panel for the first time and I have to say the training really stood to me. It was tougher than anything I did subsequently with Mick Dempsey but if I had done a lot of physical work in the barracks during the day, they wouldn't flog me at county training that night.

We'd have various tests over the course of our training, be it for marching or several weapons that we had to be able to use. Before passing out, we'd be subjected to something called 'scratch', just to really wreck our heads one last time. It could last up to four hours and we'd have to run around carrying logs, crawling through drains and mucky water. Relentless stuff.

On the whole, it was difficult but a good experience and we'd still have a bit of craic in the evenings with eight lads in the room. When it came to passing out, we got our certificate and had to put on a marching exhibition in the square. The family were all there for that and there is a sense of pride in having come through the five months. Then there was the two to three star training for 10 weeks, which was more of the same but it's moving things on a bit and is a little bit more difficult. I got a rank merit then and that made me a fully trained soldier.

I believe that joining the army helped my hurling career in terms of developing me physically for senior inter-county level and building my mental toughness. It was part of my job in the army to be fit and healthy. It allowed me to hit the gym on a Monday morning if there was nothing else going on in the barracks. There was a handball alley that I could puck around in and a swimming pool nearby in Hotel Kilkenny that I could pop over to for recovery.

Eventually, after a promotion embargo put in place in 2009 was lifted, I reached the rank of corporal. It meant I got to crack the whip on the new recruits. I enjoyed moulding them into soldiers and I'd like to think I was hard but fair with them over the years. Some of them might claim otherwise!

I finished in the army a couple of weeks after I retired from playing for Kilkenny. It wasn't as big of a wrench, I have to say, but then quitting Kilkenny hadn't exactly torn the heart and soul out of me either. I had a few weeks of annual leave to use up so I finished in the army 12 years, almost to the day, after I'd started in December 2004. It was very simple in the end. I just went into the orderly room and told them. They got the paperwork ready then. When leaving, you're required to return all of your stuff but all of mine was in my locker and I just let them have it. I didn't even have to clear it out.

On the surface, it would appear to have been quite an upheaval in my life, leaving the army and retiring from inter-county duty within a fortnight of each other having been committed to both for 12 years but I didn't really look at it like that; it's not my way. I just drew a line under both and got on with it.

############

Sunday, December 16, 2018

I had my third meeting with Kim this weekend. We've been in regular contact since the last time we saw each other and there's a strange kind of normality to the whole thing now. It's like we've always been in touch. There's no awkwardness there at all. Everything just seems to have clicked and it's like we've packed 34 years into a few months. Now, there's still a lot that we have to learn about each other's lives but, even at that, it feels like we've known each other a long time. That's highly unusual for me as I generally need to know people for a fair length of time before letting them in. Observing her kids and their mannerisms can be a bit surreal at times. 'Jesus, that's an out and out Larkin there,' I'd say to myself, particularly with Leah.

We had been planning this weekend for a while and her and Anne had been in touch to get it organised. Kim had said how she'd taken the kids to see Santa at Fota Island before and we thought we'd all do it together with our kids this year, while my father would come down with his family too. It made for 15 of us getting together, all told.

We booked into a hotel last night, had a few drinks there and then in Kim's house. We talked about stuff like her husband Khaled's salon in Cork and his other one in Dubai. How they're trying to get his visa sorted so that they can buy their own home here in Ireland. How her girls are getting on in school.

Our children get on very well with each other too. Leah hadn't been in great form the first couple of times we saw her – she's only two and a half – but she was sprightly today and was running around after Ellie. Kim's other three daughters, Shannon, Colleen and Aisling, got on well with Mark and Holly as well as my youngest brother, Allen.

This morning we had breakfast and headed to Mahon Point for a bit of shopping and I had to grab a belated birthday present for Colleen having forgotten about her big day a couple of weeks back. Then it was on to Fota Island to see Santa. We exchanged bags of presents for the kids and Anne and I got Kim a voucher for the Pembroke Hotel in Kilkenny so she can come up here some weekend and stay.

My father seems very chilled out in her company now. He has a tendency to not be himself when he's getting to know someone but, if he was like that when he first met her, he isn't now. Last night I noticed how he was leaning in and having his own chat with her while the rest of us talked away. He was sceptical about it at the start but has now let her in, which is great.

We don't have plans as such to meet up during Christmas beyond this. I suppose she's had her own routine over the years and I'm conscious of the fact that we're only after coming into her life. I don't want to be putting pressure on her either. We know we're welcome down there and she knows she's welcome up here any time and that's good enough for now. She did say how pleased she was to have found us and how satisfying it is to be able to do lovely things like we did this weekend. It's mutual.

We've missed out on a lot of Christmases together but at least this is a start.

############

My memories of my parents being together are very vague and I really have little or nothing to draw on in that respect. I was very small when their marriage ended. They married fairly young and then had me a few years later. I don't remember there being any blazing rows between them but it seems they just grew apart. My mother met someone else and eventually went on to marry him. She's told me that she just didn't love my father in the end.

I always wanted them to get back together and, in my youthful innocence, believed it was only a matter of time before they would. I remember quizzing her about it as we walked down the town one day.

'Are you going to get back together? When are you going to get back together?'

'Eoin, we're not going to get back together. These things happen with adults.'

Still, I don't ever recall being an unhappy child having come from a broken home and never felt that it had a negative impact on me but my wife, Anne, takes a different view, believing that I should have had counselling at some stage. She reckons that I've a selfish streak and that if I want to do something, I'm too quick to do it without considering her or the kids. She's probably right, in fairness, but I don't see the link between that and what happened with my parents. 'That's just the way I am,' I tell her.

There was a custody battle between my parents which got a little ugly but, in the end, I was left with my mother. My father stayed in the marital home initially before buying his own place while my mother moved around to a few different council houses before settling in the one she's in now.

For a long number of years my father was very bitter about the whole thing. Often, when my mother was working, I'd be at home with her partner and now husband, Paddy. My father would ring to talk to me and if Paddy answered the phone, he'd order me to come down to his house straight away. He really struggled with the idea of Paddy assuming his position with me.

But Paddy was always very fair with me and I couldn't say a bad word about him. Naturally, there were times that he'd have to pull me up on certain things and on one or two occasions I'd fire back at him, 'You're not my father, you can't tell me what to do!' It was a cheap shot which he didn't deserve and I'd always apologise later but, I have to say, it was very rare that we were at odds. When Louise came along it would have been easy for him to favour her given that she was his biological daughter but that never happened. We were both treated just the same. Anything she got, I did too and if not, he would have made sure I did.

Things are much better now between my parents and I'd say the catalyst was probably my father finding happiness with someone else. He's married to Veronica now and he adopted Anthony, who Veronica had before they met, and went on to have Allen together.

It's come full circle because on occasions you'd see my father and Paddy even having a drink and a laugh together in The Village Inn and my mother wouldn't even be there. It was a very gradual thing but, in ways, my hurling career may have helped to move things along, too. There were lots of matches where the tickets I'd dish out to the family would leave them all sitting in close proximity to each other. There were banquets and functions and awards nights and medal presentations that they'd all have been at.

Anthony was 22 in August, Allen only turns 12 next month, making him slightly younger than two of ours, and he knocks great fun out of that with Mark and Holly. 'You can't talk to me like that, I'm your uncle,' he tells them. It's somewhat strange in that, although I spent a lot of time in my father's house, I never really lived with Anthony or Allen, even though we're brothers. So it's different, but we're all good.

I wouldn't say that I'm closer to one parent than the other, but I have a contrasting relationship with both of them, as I'd imagine is the case for most people. I can talk to my mother about anything but, like a lot of father-son relationships, particularly in this country, my father and I don't go too deep in our conversations. If we're talking about something it wouldn't tend to stray too far beyond hurling. He'll occasionally let his guard down, however.

I remember being in Delaney's on Patrick Street one Saturday after playing a game when I was about 18 and my father came in from a work do. He was fairly full and sat down and put his arm around me. 'There he is now, the fruit of my loins.' I was mortified. 'Is this lad for real?'

It's not just drink-related when it comes to letting his emotions go, however. It was the same after winning something with the club or county over the years. 'We made him,' he blubbed to my mother the night after I lifted Liam MacCarthy in 2012. Given that he's the sort of character that largely keeps his emotions in check, I suppose it means all the more on the rare occasions that he expresses himself in that way.

My mother's different in that respect, yet similar. She'd be more open emotionally but it's only when she has a few drinks on board that she'll get into the heavy stuff. She carries guilt about leaving my father, feeling it might have impacted negatively on me and gets teary-eyed about it at times, but only when she's had a few. I always reassure her that I turned out just fine regardless and that I probably would have turned out a lot worse had I been reared in an unhappy home with the two of them.

While my father's difficulties with Paddy left me in an awkward position at times, my parents never used me as a means to hurt the other. At Christmas they always put me first. As a young lad, I'd stay in my mother's on Christmas Eve, then I'd call to my father for a while on Christmas morning before working my way around to my granny's place and one or two other legs of the family to collect presents before generally having dinner back at my mother's. I have nothing but happy memories of Christmas as a youngster despite coming from what would be described as a broken home, and my parents deserve great credit for that. In fact, I'd generally get a present from each of them where most kids would tend to get one jointly from their parents, so I was doubling my lot.

I used to get hurls nearly every Christmas and Manchester United jerseys were a regular gift too, particularly the goalkeeper ones as I used to play in goals in soccer when I was a young lad, with a pair of gloves to boot. I was never big into computer games as I tended to prefer being out and about but I did get a Sega Megadrive and another year I got a PlayStation. One year I was given an electric guitar with an amplifier. It must have cost a fortune, and what a waste it was.

I never even had lessons. Just messed around with it for a few days and left it there.

There's certainly no chip on my shoulder over my parents' situation though it's not something I talk about too much. It's just easier that way. If someone asks me how many brothers and sisters I have or something like that, I just tell them that it's two of each without adding any qualifications. For me, my family circumstances have been a normality that I've always lived comfortably with.

############

Tuesday, December 25, 2018

We all have our Christmas traditions and one of mine is common among Irish males: last-ditch shopping on Christmas Eve. It was one that I maintained yesterday as I took off into town in search of a present for Anne. Typically, I'm happy enough to let her get all the various bits and pieces for the kids and the wider family but when it came to getting something for her, I just popped in to Stevie Nolan, a jeweller, and picked up a ring. Stevie wrapped it up for me and as I left he smirked and said, 'See you this time next year, Eoin!' I just had to get some other bits and pieces and I was all done at around midday.

After that, I felt like I wanted to open out the lungs a bit. Bar going for a run with my cousin, I had done nothing since James Stephens lost the quarter-final replay two months ago. I only did half an hour up in the club but it was intense. On the rower, pulling like a dog, as the O'Donovan brothers would say, and then up on the spinning bike. I was fucked after it, though it wasn't unexpected. And, still, you're hoping that the residue of fitness that has been built up over the years would be enough to see you through.

This is the third winter since I retired from Kilkenny duty and the first one that I let myself go a bit and slipped into bad habits. The first year, I was planning to go back with Kilkenny until December so I had been looking after myself and I didn't go too mad last winter either. But this year, I ate a fair amount of rubbish and put on a bit of weight, all of which comes back to you when you're labouring on the rower or the bike. I don't tend to weigh myself and it's not even a case of being able to pinch a bit more around the belly – all I have to do is look at it. Yesterday was an eye-opener for me to pull my ears in a bit this Christmas with regard to what I put into my body.

Christmas in our house wouldn't do much for your sleep pattern, however. The kids are up at 5am every Christmas morning. I'd be happier to set their alarms a couple of hours later but Anne inists. 'Ah look, it only happens once a year, they're excited.'

So up we all got and the excitement in their faces, particularly with Ellie, the youngest, was something to behold. She got various bits and bobs but it was all about the coveted Reborn Baby doll for her before she dared to look at the other stuff. She was hyper; jumping up and down, gasping.

The elder two have moved past that stage now. Too cool to show those sort of emotions! They got plenty of stuff too though, a laptop for Holly and an iPad for Mark being the standouts. I got the usual – pyjamas and socks, a couple of vouchers that I'll use to buy some clothes in a few months' time, and a wallet thrown in as well. I called around to my father and dropped off gifts and went back to bed at about 10.30am for a few hours, then we had our dinner here in our house with my mother, Paddy and Louise coming around. We had a few drinks and they left a few hours later.

The racing kicks in tomorrow and that will help to see me through to 2019.

A1

5

JANUARY

*'We've a long year ahead of us, we've finished the
holiday, we're not All-Ireland champions anymore.
It's all about this year'*

New Zealand. Dubai and Thailand. Orlando. Miami.
Malaysia. San Francisco, San Diego and Hawaii.
Cancun. Trips we took over the years with Kilkenny.
Places where we rang in the new year, well removed from
the bleak winter back home. We'd usually jet off from Dublin
Airport a couple of days after Christmas; the odd time we'd
leave on St Stephen's Day.

Traditionally, All-Ireland finalists embark on a team holiday
so that meant that we were flying away somewhere for 10 of
the 12 years that I was involved, though I didn't go on the last
two. Generally we'd be gone for 10 days or so, though we got
just a week after losing the 2010 final to Tipperary. Needless
to say, there was a message in that.

There wouldn't be any great discussion about where we were going. We'd just be told and would run with it, though one year a few of us were talking about doing our own thing and booking a skiing trip in the Rocky Mountains. Word got back to Brian Cody and a meeting was called. 'I've heard that some of ye are trying to organise going off on your own but this is a team holiday, we're going as a team. You're not getting any vouchers, you'll come on the team holiday or you don't go at all.' So that was the end of that.

The fundraising that was required of us for these trips was fairly minimal, to be fair. We'd be given five framed photographs of the All-Ireland winning team which we'd have to sell at €50 each. I used to buy one for Anne's father and my father would often take one. I'd try and flog a couple to local publicans though you'd feel more than a bit sheepish when approaching them year after year with essentially the same product.

We used to get an allowance for the trip as well, €1,500 per couple though it later dropped to €1,000. Now, it wouldn't get you too far in fairness but it was better than a kick in the arse. In fairness to the Kilkenny county board, they always included the women, something that I know from talking to players in other counties wasn't a given elsewhere. The wives and girlfriends enjoyed the trips as much as we did. They had their own friendships that they had built up over the years. Anne came on all of the holidays and while you could bring the kids if you wanted to, you'd have to pay for them. Some would have taken the opportunity to make a family holiday out of it but we never did. Anne's mother was a great help in that regard, taking the kids off us. Of course, I'd use these trips to score brownie points given that there was a long year of hurling still to come.

'You're after travelling the world thanks to me!' I'd tell Anne.

'The shit that I have to put up with all year just to go on a holiday!' would invariably be the retort.

The destinations tended to be places you wouldn't ordinarily go to and I'm grateful to hurling that I've seen parts of the world that I most likely wouldn't have otherwise and probably won't see again. New Zealand stands out in that respect. It was the best of all the trips. All of the others were just chaos with drink but there wasn't nearly as much consumed on that one because there was so much to do and lads didn't want to be sick when doing the activities. Queenstown particularly was just epic. The amount of stuff that you could get up to. Speedboats, white water rafting, bungee jumping, skydiving. I didn't chance jumping out of a plane myself though John Tennyson did and had his stomach turned – he was as white as a ghost after it.

Thailand was a great trip too. We were being ferried around in a tuk tuk one night when the driver stopped to get out for some reason; he may have been clearing something on the road. Seán Cummins saw his chance. He jumped in the driver's seat and sped off, nearly turning the thing over and leaving the driver chasing after us waving his arms. Seán soon stopped though the driver was like a demon after it.

On the same trip, we went on the rampage on the first night and made an awful racket when we got back to the hotel in Bangkok, shouting and singing at four or five in the morning. Complaints were made and Cody called us all into a room the next day. 'You're going to have to calm down lads,' he said to us. 'You're in Thailand now. If you get arrested over here there's fuck all we can do for ye.'

Miami is another of these places that you wouldn't typically pick as a holiday destination with Irish people more likely to gravitate towards places that have a strong diaspora like New York, Boston, Chicago and San Francisco when visiting the States. It was another savage spot though. The highlight was getting to meet Edwin van der Sar, who was in the same hotel as us. People were jumping in for photographs with him and then later in the holiday we were down on the beach and ended up joining in a game of volleyball with him. Once the first couple went up, we were like sheep. It must have been 12 against 12 in the end. A day or two later we ended up messing around in the pool with him and his son and daughter playing headers.

I'm a Manchester United fan so it was nice to meet him, though it would have been a much bigger deal when I was younger. Most of us tend to grow out of our youthful fanaticism. He was pleasant, though he knew nothing about hurling. He couldn't figure out how we were amateur sportsmen, yet we'd end up on a team trip to Miami. We didn't get too deep into conversation with him and kept a respectful distance as, while none of us had a profile anything like his, we know what it's like to be badgered in public to varying degrees.

It's probably not as bad in hurling as in football given that we wear helmets, but Anne would often say to me, 'It's a disaster walking down the town with you, every Tom, Dick and Harry is stopping to ask you about Kilkenny.' The questions would usually be along the lines of, 'Well, how will you get on at the weekend?' I'd like to think I'm fairly pleasant to people in these instances, even if I could do without it at times. The nights of big games used to be the worst. You'd get off the bus and head into Langton's for the few pints, people would be in your face asking you all about the match when it's the last thing you want to talk about and you just want to enjoy your pint in peace. Other times, people think it's ok to just intrude when you're out doing something with your family.

Again, I'd be respectful and would pass it off while privately wishing they'd just move on. There's only one incident I can remember where I did get narky. I was in The Village Inn having a few drinks with friends when this chap came over with the phone to his ear before presenting it to me.

'Here, will you talk to this lad?'

'To be honest about it,' I said, 'I don't really want to talk to him now. I'm after having a good few pints.'

'Ah just talk to him for a minute...'

'No, I'm not talking to him.'

'Oh, you're as ignorant,' he said, the irony of that observation clearly lost on him.

I used to get requests like that from time to time and you wouldn't know who you could be talking to. Their cousin in America or something. It's pure cringe. But, by and large, I'd have to say that Kilkenny people are very good and wouldn't be as in-your-face as supporters in other counties.

I suppose the tradition of team holidays for All-Ireland winners or finalists started about 40 or 50 years ago when travelling overseas wasn't as accessible as it is now and it really was the opportunity of a lifetime for players. It probably doesn't carry quite the same appeal nowadays with the world a smaller place but I still think it's a great reward for players' efforts over the course of the year, not to mention the wives and girlfriends'.

It's phenomenal for team spirit because, while you train with these fellas all year, you wouldn't necessarily be chatting to them a whole pile, bar on nights out after games and even at that, you might not get a chance to talk to some. You cover far more ground with teammates on a holiday than you would for the rest of the year. The same with the training weekends, though they were never any further than Fota Island or Carton House. Brian Cody wasn't into the La Manga craze that the Armagh footballers started in 2002. We didn't need to get on a plane to train hard for a few days.

I was lucky enough to go on a few All Star trips too but the dynamic was hugely different on those. Factions would be likely to form though, I have to say, we had good craic with the Tipp lads. The Cork lads less so. They did their own thing. I was supposed to be rooming with Dan Shanahan in Singapore one year and he came up to me and announced, 'I'm going to stay with the Waterford lads, alright?'

'Grand,' I said, 'work away.'

By and large, we wouldn't see much of the management on the team holidays. The supporters' club might organise a bit of food and drink one of the nights but, outside of that, they did their own thing and you generally wouldn't mix with them. We never trained collectively on the holidays though as the years moved on you'd see fellas hitting the gym a bit. Towards the end of my career, I tried to get out for a run most days as I didn't want to be left behind by the young lads when training resumed on our return.

You'd notice some up and coming players who wouldn't have been that long on the panel minding themselves a little on the team holidays, looking for that edge to get into the team. Conor Fogarty stands out in my memory for that. He'd be in the gym. Going for a run. Trying to eat the right food. He'd still have the craic in the evening time and drink his pints but outside of that he'd be careful. The more seasoned players among us would look at lads tipping into the gym and just say, 'Nah, we'll go for a pint.'

I didn't go on the last couple of team holidays because they just didn't fit in with what was going on in my life at that time. I was in the middle of a tour of duty in 2015/16 and I'd already retired by the time the next team holiday came around the following year. Dumping the kids with our parents and heading off had become less palatable, so we got vouchers and took family holidays to Florida and Lanzarote. Last year we went to Santa Ponsa. Things we never got to do during my Kilkenny career.

We'd go out in the evening for a meal and have a couple of drinks while the kids amused themselves on the iPads. Back to the hotel or apartment at a reasonable hour then and have a few drinks that we'd bought in the supermarket out on the balcony while the kids were in bed. Simple, chilled out kind of stuff. And that's all I want now.

I've had all the holidays on the beer with 30 teammates and they were brilliant, but I'm past that and don't long for those times again. This summer we're going to Fuerteventura and I can't wait.

#

Friday, January 11, 2019

I had my three-month review in TransferMate with my team leader, Karen Brennan, today. It was largely positive. I'm pretty punctual and have applied myself reasonably well to the job considering I had no prior experience in the field. The first couple of months are really a training period so you're not being judged too harshly but she did tell me that my targets would be going up and that I'd need to bring in more business from now on.

I managed to get the Donnelly Group in Tyrone on board having first made contact with Philip Jordan some months back. As a car dealership in the North, the service we offer is ideal for them. I saw on their website that Philip was their finance director. One of the other lads had been working on them so I asked him could I step in as I reckoned the GAA connection would help. I emailed him and it went from there.

He was away on holidays at the time but when he got back we had a good chat on the phone. There wasn't much GAA talk but we did touch on how it's nice to get those family holidays that are much harder to organise when you're playing at inter-county level. Maybe we would have got them on board in any event, but I'd like to think that the GAA link that we shared certainly helped.

As it happens, it's two years this week since I started in Pfizer. Straight away I liked it. Essentially the job revolved around producing enbrel, a drug that's used to treat rheumatoid arthritis. There are various phases to it and I would have been roughly in the middle of the whole process. It was both computer-based and had a manual element. We'd upload the different phases, like cleaning or steaming, into the system on the computer. There were these massive vessels in which media, a feed that enables protein cells to grow, was placed and after they're moved on to the next phase, we'd have to clean and steam the vessels for the next batch coming through. Like a lot of things, it was challenging at the start and then it just becomes routine.

Shortly after I started there, my brother Anthony expressed an interest in applying for a job there and I told him to go for it. He got in there and though he worked in a different area to me, we worked the very same shifts so we shared a lift up and down to Saggart together with James Holden, which helped to break the monotony.

We were listening to *Beat 102-103* one morning, wrecked after a 12-hour shift, when Anthony decided to take part in the 'Beat The Bomb' quiz. It was typical of Anthony's humour to do something like that though, as Larry Gogan used to say, the questions didn't quite suit him and James and I were in stitches in the car beside him.

However, after a little over a year into the job, it began to get on top of me. Not the actual work itself, but the fact that I was working shifts and then the commute on top of it. Initially, I was sleeping fine. I could come in after a night shift and fall into a coma and the night before I'd go back on days I'd sleep soundly too.

But the longer I did it, the more my body clock fell out of sync. I was becoming increasingly tired. Wrecked. It got to a stage where I couldn't sleep after being on nights and then when the day shifts would come around, I'd be staring at the ceiling at 3am when I had to be up at 10 to five to get to work for 6.45am. I was like a zombie going around the place. I was narky at home. My mood dropped and darkened. I knew I had to find something else.

#

We mostly didn't start collective training until we returned from the team holiday in early January. We would have had fitness tests and been on gym programmes before Christmas but we only trained in December if it was a year in which we had failed to win the All-Ireland. Cody's way of reminding us that we'd fallen short the previous season, I suppose. Training the wrong side of Christmas is difficult psychologically. Trying to get your diet right to allow you to train properly was tough at that time of year. It's very hard to motivate yourself for it.

It's not a bed of roses in bleak January either but it's a new calendar year and you're looking firmly forward, not back. At some stage in January, Cody would address us. I wouldn't call it a speech as such, but he'd often let training roll out for a week or two and then there'd be a meeting called at some stage during that month. We'd all know exactly what would be coming. 'We've a long year ahead of us, we've finished the holiday, we're not All-Ireland champions anymore. It's all about this year.'

I'd approach it thinking, *what's he going to say that he hasn't said any other year?* And yet I'd always walk out with a spring in my step after he'd managed to put a different slant on things yet again. I'd be half pumped. 'Yeah, we'll give it a good stab again this year and see where we get to.'

That's Brian at his best. His single greatest attribute is his ability to refocus players and instil a fresh hunger despite the success we had enjoyed as a group.

We'd often have a Walsh Cup game to face into a few days after stepping off the plane. I played in a lot of them in the early part of my career though when my hip and groin problems started to flare up I was largely excused. The slogging that went with hurling that early in the year was not going to serve me well later in the season so I'd be allowed to focus on prehab and rehab instead.

But when I did play in those Walsh Cup matches, they were a complete pain in the arse. Hurling in January is just a disaster, really.

Typically, you'd have very little hurling done so your touch would be all over the place, while we wouldn't have got through much physical work at that stage either. Yet, we generally tended to do well in the Walsh Cup and won it pretty regularly during my time. It goes back to the dynamic within the panel. Lads were mad to get in the Kilkenny team and it was easier to get in there in January, play well and stay there rather than hoping to make a late run in the league or for the Championship. It just doesn't work like that generally.

A shitty Walsh Cup match in Freshford would be what Conor Fogarty and others like him were eyeing when they weren't going as hard as the rest of us out in the sun a week or two before. If you're after having a good Walsh Cup and carry it into the league, it's going to be hard for Brian to drop you when the more established players come back. And the stalwarts that were already there were chomping at the bit to keep them out too.

Leabharlann na Cabra
Cabra Library
Tel: 8691414

After all, most lads' careers start in the Walsh Cup, though I was an exception. I made my Kilkenny senior debut in late March 2005 owing to James Stephens' club run. It was a transitional period and a good time for me to be coming in; I slotted straight in after the club campaign. I don't think I could have done that in 2006 or 2007 when we were starting to accumulate All-Irelands.

I used to hear horror stories from other teams and the training they'd be doing. 'Why are we not doing this kind of training?' I'd wonder. 'Why are we not being dogged like that?' Now, it used to be hard, don't get me wrong, but generally it would be just one night of really hard training a week, on a Tuesday.

On the Friday night then we'd have drills and a bit of ball work, then a league or Walsh Cup match most weekends. If there was no match, we'd fit in another hard session. We had residual fitness in the bank but we'd build ourselves up gradually over the spring and a few weeks after the league final I'd feel as if, 'Yeah, we're on the level now again.'

In the early years, our training would start in St Kieran's College, on the old soccer pitch which had a big incline. We'd run up that hill and by the time you'd get back around to the bottom to run up it again, the mud would have thickened and as the night wore on you felt like your legs were being pulled from the sockets. We'd use Kilkenny College for hard running too.

Both places had gyms where we'd do our weight sessions as well. On a Friday night we'd use Fennessy's Field in Kieran's for some hurling drills or we might go to Ballyragget. By and large the facilities weren't hectic. The lighting wouldn't have been great, for example, and the showers could be cold some nights.

I wouldn't say that Brian Cody revelled in us training in facilities that were relatively substandard for character-building purposes because in later years we had a training ground built in Dunmore and a fine gym installed in Nowlan Park. But no player would be volunteering to tell him the showers were cold at the same time. It's probably just a cultural thing in Kilkenny. We got on with things. Would the Cork players have kicked up a stink over something like that?

Most years we were quite strong in the league, some we weren't. There was never any policy shift coming from the management to the players in terms of how we approached the competition. There was never an address along the lines of, 'If we win the league, great, but we want to make sure we're in top condition for the summer.' Maybe a conversation along those lines took place with the management behind closed doors but the message to the players never wavered – go out to win every game. Maybe some years you'd have a few more inexperienced players dropped into the team, though never would there be a suggestion that we wouldn't take a game or the competition seriously.

But there was a creeping intensity to Cody as the year wore on. In the winter, the only time you'd hear his voice on the field was when things might slacken off a little. Other than that you'd barely know he was there, wrapped up in his wet gear and wooly hat. In the early season gym sessions, he'd pop in for a few minutes, dressed in a pair of jeans, perhaps. If you didn't know who he was, you'd be wondering what he was doing there. He'd just drift in and out, happy to let Mick

Dempsey set the temperature. In the summer, it's different. Cody's in the thick of it. He has the peak cap and the polo top on, in the middle of everything you're doing, bellowing away. That's the subconscious trigger for you to step it up.

His trust in Mick to get us right physically was absolute. This is a man, remember, whose sporting background was wrapped up entirely in Laois football, so he would have been viewed suspiciously in Kilkenny. He was living in the city and worked with some club football teams before being brought into the under-21 hurling set up and then Brian promoted him to the seniors. His lack of hurling pedigree became irrelevant once players realised that he knew what he was at. Perhaps it took a couple of years to realise he was quite competent and then another couple to surmise he was excellent. 'There's no team going to be fitter than us or better conditioned than us because there's no one better than Mick Dempsey at doing what he does,' Cody would regularly tell us.

It was easy to believe him. We were always as fit, if not fitter, than any team we played against but, and this is the crucial thing, we were fresh as well. He didn't want to run us into the ground and leave us stale when the big days came around.

In fairness, how often have you seen Kilkenny teams flag in the last 10 minutes of matches? It just didn't happen. I defy anyone to say that any big game we lost over the years was down to a lack of physical fitness. Mick had it down to a tee. Maybe every three weeks during the summer we'd do a bit of running to top up our fitness but he was always very conscious of balancing that with rest and recovery so that we'd be hopping out of our skins come match day, which we invariably were.

Sunday, January 27, 2019

It's more than two years now since I last played for Kilkenny and I'll be 35 this summer. Suffice to say, my training schedule isn't quite what it used to be and I feel it needs to be tailored a little to allow me to get another few years of playing with the club. I've been doing a bit since my blowout on Christmas Eve. I'm going to the gym at lunchtime most days this January; Hotel Kilkenny is just over the road.

I can't just go back to train with the club starting from scratch; I need to get myself at least somewhat fit to be able to train. But I intend on talking to the management about my own schedule as I don't believe that it will serve me well to go through all the slogging that typically goes with early season training, particularly given my historical groin and hip problems.

It's funny though, here's me talking about easing myself back in and then you have Michael 'Brick' Walsh, who's a year older than me, already back in the thick of it with Waterford for another year, playing pre-season games and he featured against Offaly in the first round of the league today. But, in ways, it's easier for him because he's stayed at that level. If you're playing at a certain level and then drop down, it's much more difficult to get back up there when you're getting on. It's far easier to do that in your mid-20s.

I'd imagine Brick is the sort of player that Brian Cody would have loved. There's no bullshit about him, he just wants to come in and train hard, improve himself, prepare properly and perform as well as he possibly can for the team. The Cody doctrine. There's no banging the chest and kissing the crest like there was with some of his teammates over the years. They took fist-pumping to a new level too though I can't say too much about that as I was partial to the odd one myself!

How would Brian have managed the more, shall we say, flamboyant Waterford hurlers like John Mullane, Dan Shanahan and Eoin Kelly? While they were outstanding players for Waterford, they couldn't have survived in Cody's environment with the type of persona they carried throughout their careers. They would certainly have been given an opportunity and it would have been up to them after that. Of course, there's every chance that they would have been shaped by the culture that Cody created and adapted accordingly. Others did.

There were plenty of players that came into the Kilkenny set up over the years, however, that were far more talented than I was but they just didn't have the mindset for it and were let go.

Cha Fitzpatrick may have had a reputation as a lad who could take or leave hurling given that he retired when he was just 27 but his head was right when he started hurling with Kilkenny and he gave it his all.

He was probably just a victim of the game moving in a different direction. After we lost to Tipperary in 2010, Brian seemed to conclude that we needed physical power in midfield and when he couldn't get a look-in in 2011, the writing was on the wall for him really.

John Mulhall was one who probably had a little too much of a circus around him. He was a great fella and a fine hurler, there was no badness in him at all and he would have been dedicated but the craic just probably got the better of him.

He loved it too much. Brian would have been at the end of his tether with him sometimes. We were playing Dublin in Parnell Park once and while Brian was happy for me to roam around and follow the ball, he gave John strict instructions to just play his own position.

'I want you to play half-forward, win that position and stay there. Do you understand that now? Am I after making myself clear?'

'Yeah, yeah, I understand it, yeah.

'Are you sure now? Am I after making myself absolutely clear?'

He must have gone through it with him about four times just to be sure. Then the ball had barely been thrown in and John was over on the other side of the field. Cody lost the rag and whipped him off before half-time. Then there was the song that he sang at the homecoming after the 2011 All-Ireland which was derogatory towards Tipperary.

'Now we've taken back our throne/Tipperary póg mo thóin/ Liam MacCarthy's comin' fuckin' home…'

Cody soon stepped in and announced to the crowd that 'you've probably just witnessed a performance by a fella who is probably going to have the shortest inter-county career of all-time'. He didn't last much longer.

#

We had our first meeting with Séamas 'Cheddar' Plunkett, our new manager, this morning. I was immediately very impressed by him. He doesn't seem to say anything without having thought about it. He doesn't just let his tongue run away on him, spewing out cheap soundbites. You can see how much it means to him to take on this job and, despite saying he won't be with us full-time until the summer, I'd don't imagine he'll be missing too much.

We met him in small groups and I went in with Matthew Ruth and Jackie Tyrrell. He was curious as to why we lose games to teams that, on paper, we ought to be beating. I said that I didn't feel we were pushing ourselves as hard as we could and that we take breaks in games and lose concentration too easily. Jackie then turned the question back on him, asking him what he feels we need to do in order to kick on. He thought about it and said, 'I don't think I can answer that at the moment because I don't know enough about the lads. It'll take me a good few weeks to get to know them and get to know their personality, what way they train and what way they conduct themselves on and off the field.'

He pointed out how we're back down at the bottom of the pile setting out in 2019. He told us all that he'll make certain demands and if they're not met, he'll be pointing it out. 'Ye'll only get one chance and if ye don't pull up your socks and give us what we want, you're no good to us.'

I spoke to Seamus Dwyer, our coach, about my own training schedule and how I felt I needed to mind myself a little at this stage of the year with the business end of the season in mind. 'You won't be doing everything,' Séamus told me, 'we'll be managing the older lads' sessions. You'll be doing 75 percent of the session.'

This afternoon, I went to Nowlan Park to see Kilkenny play Cork in the first game of the league. Kilkenny won easily by seven points though, I have to say, Cork were atrocious.

Kilkenny didn't particularly impress either. Huw Lawlor became the latest to audition for the troublesome full-back role and he struggled a bit with Aidan Walsh. The latest Tommy Walsh from Tullaroan hurled well at corner-back and Conor Delaney was probably their best player at wing-back, scoring two points.

Bar Cormac Murphy, who was decent in midfield, Cork offered nothing. They were that bad that it reminded me of the famous league game in 2009 when they came up to Nowlan Park on the back of their third strike. We gave them a right going over that day.

#

There was no great love for Cork in our dressing room back then, to put it mildly. To us, they were full of shit. Now, the county board in Kilkenny was a dream to work with and, by and large, we got everything we wanted. But we didn't seek to have our towels folded and waiting for us when we came in from training and that kind of nonsense. We didn't insist on trimmings that are incidental to winning hurling matches.

Donal Óg Cusack and his special contact lenses and glove for catching the ball was more of it. He once said how he went out on his bike one Christmas Day to try and get an edge on the hurlers all over Ireland that were full up with turkey.

What edge was he getting going out for a cycle? Maybe the lads that were at home enjoying themselves with their families were the ones that were really getting the edge. They were unwinding at Christmas time and guarding against being mentally stale later in the year. You had Seán Óg Ó hAilpín going out for a run the morning after they won an All-Ireland. Grand, he doesn't take a drink but, Jesus, take a break, will you?

Someone told me how they even had the design of their shorts changed at one stage with 'Corcaíoch', Irish for 'Corkman', woven into them. Why would something like that even come into your head? Just put on a pair of shorts and go out and play the game, for God's sake.

We turned them over in the 2006 All-Ireland final and that was the end of them. They really hit their peak in 2005 and were on a downward spiral after that. They only had maybe 17 players that were quality inter-county hurlers and many of them had been on the go for a long time at that stage. A lot of things kicked off in Cork after 2006 but I don't think it stopped them winning further All-Irelands; they just weren't good enough anymore. We beat them comfortably in the 2008 semi-final and even more so at the same stage two years later.

In between there was that league game in Nowlan Park. When the strike had finished up a few weeks before it, a comment came out of their camp that if it hadn't been for all the strife, it would be them going for four-in-a-row that year instead of us. Thinking it is one thing, but to have the arrogance to come out and say it was another. You just don't get comments like that coming out of Kilkenny. That played into our hands.

We didn't go out with the attitude to give them a good hiding that day, but there was a determination that they absolutely couldn't come up and beat us in Nowlan Park after all that had gone on. They were the antithesis of what we were about.

You could feel it in the build-up to the game around Kilkenny; it was like what you'd experience before a big championship match. Our people were leaving us in no doubt as to what was expected of us. They were with us throughout the game too. We never looked at the scoreboard and neither did they.

When the fourth goal went in, they greeted it like it was the winner. We were so focused on beating them that we just kept going and going and going. We had a standing ovation at half-time and again at the end, by which time we had 27 points to spare.

It was a surreal afternoon, all told, but a very satisfying one.

6

FEBRUARY

*'For the vast majority of my life it was just
a vague word that, as far as I was concerned,
didn't really relate to me. It was something that
other people suffered from. Strangers that you'd
just hear about'*

Friday, February 1, 2019

'There was no job satisfaction in it for me. I'm sure for certain lads there is. In the army itself, there's nothing to do. It's obviously a good thing there's nothing to do army-wise. But walk down to the locker rooms and you see lads there doing nothing, because there's nothing to do.

When I hear the nurses coming out and asking for more pay, I can see exactly why.

– Colin Fennelly.

Colin Fennelly's ears are burning this morning. He did a range of interviews yesterday ahead of Ballyhale Shamrocks' All-Ireland club semi-final and lambasted the Defence Forces, which he left last year to take up a career in project management. Is the army perfect? Absolutely not. But do I agree with what Colin said? Absolutely not.

There are plenty of opportunities for people in the Defence Forces. I did a hell of a lot in there, certainly more than I would have done had I gone down most other career paths. I definitely wouldn't have gone back and sat my Leaving Cert had it not been for the army. I did any amount of courses while in the army to better myself and broaden my skill set. If the will is there, there are more than enough opportunities that you can grasp to fill your time. Clearly Colin just went in with the attitude of serving his time and getting the hell out of it.

Moreover, his comments have undermined his former colleagues and friends, people that looked after him when he was in the army and hurling with Kilkenny. Because the money in the army is so poor, many of those that have children have to apply for a family income supplement because they just can't live on the wages. It's not going to be any easier for them to get that top-up after this outburst. Furthermore, PDFORRA, the army representative body, has been trying to claw back pay cuts imposed on soldiers back in 2008. Their bargaining position is considerably weaker today than it was 24 hours ago.

Members of the Defence Forces are asked to do an awful lot for a pittance. Maybe €7 extra for 24-hour duties. If you're coming from Wexford to Kilkenny for one of those shifts, it's going to cost you a lot more than €7 in fuel. For tours of duty there are three months of training beforehand and then the tour itself, which is six months. You might make up to €15,000 and, while that's grand if you've no attachments, is it worth it over nine months when you're not seeing your family? The government takes a slice of that in tax now as well, which didn't used to be the case.

Obviously if you work your way up your salary increases but not dramatically and they obviously can't promote everyone. I was a corporal when I left and even if I stayed at that rank for the rest of my career, I wouldn't have reached €30,000 a year. If I became a sergeant, it would only be about a tenner extra a week. And I'd have to do 16 weeks in The Curragh to achieve that rank without my fuel being covered. When I went to Pfizer, my money jumped by about €20,000 straight away. On that basis, it was an easy decision to leave. The last I heard, they were only on around €320 a week coming out of recruit training. One chap that I trained was living in Wexford and car-pooling to the barracks in Kilkenny. When the lads he was travelling with went overseas, he had to start taking annual leave because he couldn't afford to put petrol in the car and drive up on his own.

People might say, 'Sure why pay them more? They do fuck all. It's not like they're in combat. What difference would it make if they weren't there?' Doing fuck all hasn't been an impediment to any amount of people getting obscene money in this country for God knows how long. There are plenty of them in Leinster House. What does the President do, when it comes down to it, for the money he's on? He signs various bills into law and gets some lovely trips overseas. But when there's flash flooding and heavy snowfall and other dangers posed to public safety with increasingly common extreme weather events, what happens? The army is called in.

My phone has been hopping with texts and calls all day about what Colin said, not to mention people that I've bumped into asking me about it. The army have been issuing responses refuting what he said but they're on the back foot. They have to respond but, ultimately, it's Colin's comments that will leave a much greater residue.

Personally, I've always had a good relationship with Colin, he's a grand lad. But I think he's wrong on this one and he's let a lot of former colleagues down. As well as the army, he hasn't done Ballyhale or the Kilkenny team any favours by drawing this attention on himself and I'd imagine he'll be hearing from Henry Shefflin or Brian Cody about it. Or both.

Sunday, February 3, 2019

Perhaps I shouldn't be too hard on Colin. I know what it's like to suffer a public backlash. Kilkenny lost to Clare in Ennis today. The last time that happened, two years ago this month, I was in my cousin's house watching it on TV. Seething.

It was only two months after my retirement and obviously I knew all the lads involved, so it was all still a bit fresh. They lost by 13 points, the biggest defeat in all of Brian Cody's years in charge. I whipped out my phone and went straight to Twitter:

Not good enough from Kk. Still reliant on experienced lads.

Younger lads need to have the attitude, NEVER give up. Too many standing around.

Well, my phone was on fire for the rest of the evening. If I had left it for an hour, I probably wouldn't have posted it but my emotions just got the better of me. I don't regret the sentiment but I shouldn't have expressed it on social media. Granted, the team had lost a lot of experience and was in transition but I felt they allowed Clare to just walk all over them. They took everything that Clare threw at them and gave nothing back. Yes, they're young lads and they'll have learned from the experience but there's only so much you can allow yourself to be pushed around regardless of what age you are. You can be beaten because you're not good enough or because you're not doing the work that's required and it veered too much towards the latter in that game for my liking. Way too much.

There was a bit of a blowback from some clowns on Twitter and generally it wouldn't have gone down well. I went on Newstalk's *Off The Ball* the following night to explain myself. I was chatting to Jackie at club training shortly afterwards. 'Look, I know where you're coming from but maybe Twitter wasn't the right place to throw it out,' he said.

I didn't hear from Brian Cody on it. At least not straight away. When they won the league unexpectedly last year, I met him a few days afterwards.

'Did you see the match the other day?'

'Oh I did, yeah, great win.'

'I hope you put up a tweet about that!' he smiled.

We were blessed with a lot of quality hurlers during my time with Kilkenny but you can have talented players that lack consistency, who don't realise that every day they go out they have to produce. That's where mental toughness comes in and it was seriously lacking that day in Ennis and to a degree today as well, though they only lost by a point. It was flattering, however. Clare were much the better side. While they are missing key men up front, I feel they're still a bit mentally soft. I wonder if that's a wider societal issue too though, that young lads are wired that bit differently nowadays. Still, if Kilkenny can get some players back and develop that mental toughness, I think they can be formidable this year.

Thursday, February 14, 2019

Valentine's night with Tommy Walsh. Don't worry, Anne and Tommy's wife Marlis were there too! It's a tradition that the four of us go out together on Valentine's night over the past 10 years or so. Anne and Marlis hit it off a long way back.

One year I think the women got talking about how they were going for a meal on Valentine's night and we ended up going out together and it's largely been maintained ever since. It's usually just three courses, no drink, have a good chat, catch up with each other and off home. We went to Butcher, a new restaurant in Kilkenny, though I could only have a starter and then I had to head off to training. It's a pity as I wouldn't see Tommy a whole lot these days, but we were saying we must get the crew together again soon.

Tommy is one of my closest friends from my time with Kilkenny, along with Jackie Tyrrell, JJ Delaney, Aidan Fogarty, Brian Dowling, David Herity, Michael Rice and Brian Hogan. He's one of the most skilful I ever played with and certainly the most determined. He'd be obsessive about his direct opponents. I remember the morning after we won the All-Ireland semi-final against Waterford in 2011, I called over to his house with Anne and he was still half cut from the night before when he produced a bottle of tomato ketchup.

'I'm going to squirt it all over Bonner Maher and I'm going to ate him alive!' he says.

Tommy was hardy too. He lacked height but more than compensated for it. His catching technique was just phenomenal. How often did you see him outfox lads that had several inches on him? He'd catch it anywhere, something I know better than most given how often we marked each other in training. He was right-handed so he'd catch with the left and have his right hand on the back of your helmet so you'd have your head down. There'd be little flicks across your hurl to move it out of the way but it was so subtle how he did it; you'd barely know it was happening.

There were countless times when the ball would be dropping between us and I'd think, 'Right, I definitely have this' and then, in a flash, Tommy would be gone up the field with it. It got to a stage where I just stopped competing. I would back into him so he wouldn't be able to catch the ball and let it hit the ground instead. Then you'd have a chance.

He wasn't pacey but had a great burst over 10 yards; better than mine anyway, which wouldn't be saying much. He played in various positions but eventually settled at wing-back, where he produced his best hurling. He was just a really good defender and swept up right across the half-back line and supported his full-back line too.

I generally played on the opposite side of the field to him

and he arced plenty of diagonal deliveries in my direction, always deadly accurate.

A number of the lads used to slag me, telling me that I was Cody's pet and Tommy was chief among them. 'You get away with more than most of us,' I'd be told. I'm not sure how it started; maybe it was because I wasn't exactly setting the world on fire during my first couple of years on the panel but still held my place. I remember in 2011, I was going through a horrendous run of form in training coming up to the opening championship match against Wexford. I was feeling a bit sorry for myself over it and Brian called me out before a team meeting one evening.

'What's wrong with you?'

'Ah, I just can't find a bit of form or anything.'

'You'll probably be playing full-forward, how do you feel about that?'

'Look, I don't mind where I'm playing,' I lied. I always hated playing full-forward with my back to goal and I was never the quickest to turn.

'Am I going to have to get a psychologist in for you?!' Brian wondered.

'No, I'll be grand, I'll be grand.'

I got some slagging after that. 'He wouldn't pull anyone else out like that!' I suppose Brian and I hit it off to a greater degree than he did with other players. We were able to talk to each other that little bit more. When we meet now, up in the club or somewhere like that, we'll have a chat but it wouldn't drag out too long either. The panic isn't there anymore when I talk to him, that fear of saying something that might be misinterpreted. I always measured every word when speaking to him as my manager. Now I can just talk freely with him. But his pet? No, I wouldn't go that far. Peter Barry was the pet when I first joined the panel and, the thing is, when Peter retired, it became Tommy. Brian absolutely loved Tommy. He'd often reference him when talking to us as an example for all to follow. Indeed, Tommy was the only player I ever saw him show real compassion for when he was dropped. And Brian dropped a hell of a lot of brilliant hurlers over the years.

Tommy just couldn't keep his place in 2014 and when we were in Langton's the night after winning the All-Ireland that year, I bumped into Brian.

'How's the other lad?' he asked me.

'Ah he's grand,' I told him.

'Ah sure look,' says Brian, 'it's hard on him, but what can you do?'

Now, it mightn't seem like much of a statement but coming from Brian Cody, it was really something. He loved everything about Tommy as a hurler and while I wouldn't go as far as to say it broke his heart to leave him out, it was probably a more difficult call with him than it was with anyone else.

It was easier for the fact that it was done from early in the year, though, when Tommy had struggled in a couple of league games and was replaced. I remember watching him in Nowlan Park one day and it was like he was standing off, not the fiery Tommy Walsh that just tore into everything. He did work his way back into the team in the forwards later that year but it didn't last. Once he wasn't getting in at wing-back, it was going to be very difficult for him to nail down a spot anywhere else.

And Tommy would have known himself where he was at. 'You know I'm finishing up now?' he said to me on the homecoming night.

'Will you shut up!' I fired back.

'No, I always said it,' he insisted, 'when you're gone, you're gone and that's it.'

He could have come back the following year and maybe played a bit here and there and picked up another medal but that wouldn't be him at all. There would have been no hard feelings on Tommy's part towards Brian either. He knew he had to do a job and Tommy wouldn't be that sort of fella anyway. The blow of losing his place would have been softened by the fact that, come the end of 2014, his brother Pádraig had taken ownership of the number five jersey.

Saturday, February 16, 2019

Our annual club fundraiser, 'For the Love of The Village', was held in the Newpark Hotel last night. This year it was a fashion show. Last year it was a lip sync, another year it was ballroom dancing.

Thankfully I managed to avoid taking part in those, but I was roped into modelling some clobber last night, which I could just about manage. All in all, it was a huge success. More than 650 attended with Marty Morrissey and Evanne Ní Chuilinn running the show.

Jackie was one of the main organisers but – believe it or not – didn't actually strut his stuff on the catwalk.

He did a lot of work behind the scenes though to make the night the success it was. Through his partnership with Littlewoods, Jackie sourced the clothes that the men wore, while a good few of the shops around town got involved as well. I was given a nice suit and had to wear a flat cap with it, something that I probably wouldn't have the balls to don ordinarily, though I like them. We had to hand the threads back anyway. After all, I have enough suits.

A spiel was prepared for every participant and Marty and Evanne did a fine job. The night was broken up by a Cilla Black-style Blind Date show and some dancers. We had to be there at 7.30pm and I was one of the last on so I had a fair bit of Heineken in me by the time I hit the catwalk; remaining vertical was the height of my ambitions. There was a mother and son theme to it so Ma took part in the fashion show and Anne did too. The same with Conor Browne and his mother, Angela Downey, the Kilkenny camogie legend, and so on.

You'd hope that nights like this can bring us closer as a club, that we can harness the goodwill around it and achieve our potential on the field later in the year. I got a bit of an earful from one of the young lads which caught me on the hop somewhat. I'm not usually too shy or retiring when it comes to pointing out where I feel we're falling short and it probably rubs some people up the wrong way. I got the feeling from this chap that he reckons I think I can say what I want because I have a few All-Irelands, which is certainly not the case. Anyway, these type of conversations are best avoided with drink on board. I was in ribbons by the time I hit the bed in the small hours of this morning but there was a very sobering conversation for me earlier in the night.

I was at the bar when I was approached by a girl who introduced herself as someone who knew Niall Donohue, the Galway hurler who took his own life in October 2013, just over a year after we had marked each other in the drawn and replayed All-Ireland finals. It was the pinnacle of my career as I lifted the MacCarthy Cup as captain. Sadly, it proved to be the high point of his, too.

She remembered how we had been direct opponents and that a few of us had been down to Kilbeacanty for the wake. She asked me what I thought of him as a hurler, things like that. It was a little intense and one thing she said in particular struck me: 'Nobody thought there was anything wrong.'

I think about Niall a lot more than she might imagine.

##

Depression. For the vast majority of my life it was just a vague word that, as far as I was concerned, didn't really relate to me. It was something that other people suffered from. Strangers that you'd just hear about. It didn't affect me or anybody I knew. How naive I was.

I'm not sharing any of this so that I can be called a hero or be described as brave. If anything I say about my experience helps people, then that's obviously fine, but I'm not necessarily doing it for that reason.

I'm not remotely interested in holding myself up as a champion for those who suffer from mental health issues. That's not me. You see people from time to time coming out with long spiels on social media about whatever issues they may have and I often wonder are they doing it as much for the endorphin-rush that goes with the likes and replies and shares and retweets as much as anything else. I'm sure many people are genuine and that it's therapeutic for them but with some, it's almost as if they're longing for some sort of cheap validation.

This is different.

I'm writing a book and my struggle with depression is an important part of my story, so it would be remiss of me not to document it. It's as simple as that.

Depression is an emotion that we all feel from time to time. You can be depressed at losing a match. Depressed at being stuck in traffic. Because your computer crashes. Then there's depression, the condition, that some of us suffer from. And I have suffered from that. Deeply, at times. Saying that is something that I have no difficulty with now but it took a hell of a long time before I reached that point. For years, Anne insisted that I was depressed but I always dismissed it out of hand. No, not me. That might happen to others, but not me. It's incredible when I think of it because I now know that everything pointed to it. Mercifully, the penny dropped in time. Otherwise, there's every chance I would have ended up as another horrible statistic.

While I rejected Anne's prompts to have myself seen to, I expected her to listen to me when the roles were reversed. After our eldest daughter Holly was born in February 2006, Anne suffered from postnatal depression, as many women unfortunately do. 'Go to the doctor,' I'd tell her. She eventually did and got better.

It was some time after Anne recovered that my mood began to drop. It was a gradual thing that crept up on me.

It wasn't that I was down in the dumps every minute of every day, but from around 2010 or so there were little things that Anne would have picked up on. I could be grand but then I'd snap about something trivial like the dishes not being in the dishwasher. The milk or the butter being left out. The kids would feel the sharpness of my tongue from time to time as well, just for being kids. Like a lot of Irish males, expressing contrition wouldn't be one of my stronger points, which would only make things worse at home.

It gradually got in on me over time. Again, I say this from my current vantage point; I was oblivious to it at the time. Or maybe, on some level, I just wanted to be oblivious. There was no catalyst for it in my everyday life. At least not an obvious one.

The army wasn't perfect but it wasn't a source of unhappiness, while I was a part of a hurling team that was continually ripping up the record books. I guess I was a high-functioning depressive. Of course there were great times in the midst of all this – lifting the MacCarthy Cup being an obvious example – but the mood swings were never too far away.

During one poor run of form hurling-wise I started seeing Brother Damien Brennan after Jackie had suggested it and passed his number on to me. Brother Damien, who was a remarkable man and was the principal at Callan CBS, is someone that Jackie swore by and he had a huge influence on him and other Kilkenny players too, to varying degrees. I was sceptical enough about seeing him initially but I concluded that it couldn't do any harm either. I would have been doing this in the context of trying to rediscover my form on the field rather than confronting my depression, however.

'When I watch you hurling,' he told me, 'it's like you're trying to please everyone bar yourself.'

He thought my body language on the field was poor and he certainly helped me to believe in myself and enjoy my hurling more than I had been. We'd chat about various things, it wouldn't be just about hurling. He'd stretch me out a bit to loosen my hips or whatever and the hour would fly by.

I went to him for a few years and while it helped, I didn't fully buy into it, though that was no reflection on Brother Damien. It's just where I was at that time, refusing to entertain the notion that I could be suffering from depression so anything that Brother Damien and I talked about was really only scratching the surface.

I was very adept at hiding my depression and Anne was the only person that picked up on it because she was exposed to me more than anyone else. My parents wouldn't even have noticed. It's a shame that I didn't engage more with Brother Damien – or that I simply wasn't able to at that time – as it would likely have spared me a lot of trauma.

Over the years there were periods when I would really resent going to training. I'd always go, but it would take quite the effort for me to get my gear together and head for Nowlan Park. This could go on for a couple of weeks. I couldn't get out of there fast enough. Naturally, my performance levels at training would drop as a result. If my touch was off or I wasn't getting the breaks I'd be particularly frustrated, to an irrational degree.

By and large I got away with these dips in form, though I was benched for the Leinster semi-final against Dublin in 2010. The management's way of sending me a message, I suppose. But then I'd snap out of it and would throw myself into training for the next couple of months before it would return. And the more it did, the longer it tended to last. The more I think of it now, I don't know how I kept going.

'You're depressed,' Anne would say, 'just go to the doctor.'

'No, I'm not going to the fucking doctor, there's nothing wrong with me.'

Eventually, I relented just to get her off my back but I clearly wasn't doing it for the right reasons, so it was a waste of time. I didn't go near Tadhg Crowley, the Kilkenny team doctor, as I didn't want to bring any of that sort of stuff into the set up. Anne explained to the doctor what I had been like to live with and I just sat there going through the motions.

'I don't think I'm depressed,' I told him, 'but Anne does.'

'Look,' he said, 'I'll prescribe you this medication and see how you feel in a couple of weeks.'

So I did as he said for a couple of weeks and then I just stopped. Anne got on my back again.

'You're not taking your tablets, you need to go back to the doctor.' I didn't.

I just carried on for several years afterwards. Allowing a creeping depression to drag me down.

##

Sunday, February 24, 2019

It's funny how your life moves on. Today, Manchester United and Liverpool were playing at Old Trafford and I arranged with a few friends and cousins to go for a few pints and watch it. It overlapped with the Tipperary-Kilkenny league game in Thurles. The hurling was on at the far end of the pub so I didn't see any of it. In other circumstances, I might have gone down to the game but I simply just wanted to go out and enjoy a few pints more than I wanted to go to Thurles.

I wasn't at all confident of a Kilkenny victory, particularly after the beating that Limerick gave them last weekend. That was an eye-opener. Limerick disposed of them with such ease and looked like they had another couple of gears too. Do Kilkenny have that? You'd seriously have to doubt it, even though they still have key players to come back. But, for all the reservations I'd have, at least they're still keeping Tipperary under the thumb. When you looked at the two line-ups today, there's no way Tipperary should have been beaten, yet Kilkenny emerged with a one-point win which goes to show yet again how the black and amber jersey spooks Tipp.

I wonder about Tipp bringing Liam Sheedy back, and I see that Eamon O'Shea has rejoined their set-up too. Sheedy did a fine job first time round but that doesn't guarantee anything. I thought they might have gone for a fresh face like Liam Cahill or Willie Maher, lads that have done well with underage teams in the last few years, just as Sheedy had before he got the job first time around.

There just seems to be something lacking down there. Over my time, they'd beat us once every few years but they'd struggle to back it up. They haven't beaten Kilkenny since the 2016 All-Ireland final, when they tore us asunder. That should have been their cue to hammer it home every time they met Kilkenny since, because that's exactly what we'd have done.

7
—

MARCH

*'For a lot of lads, that would be an
exit-stage-left moment, but that never
actually occurred to me'*

Monday, March 4, 2019

I spent twelve years in the Defence Forces and now, a little over two years after leaving, I find myself starting my third different job. It all happened so quickly. This time last week I was still an employee of TransferMate. I was on a mailing list for one of those recruitment websites and got an email about a sales job in Kilkenny Carlow Local Radio.

It's very straightforward to apply and I actually did it all on the phone there and then, just uploaded the CV and sent it off. I thought no more about it until I got an email from *KCLR*'s general manager, Pat Gardiner, who was looking to meet up with me. I arranged to meet him last Friday week in

149

the Pembroke Hotel but the night before that came around, I got a text from John Purcell, *KCLR*'s chief executive. My application had gone above Pat and now John wanted to meet with me.

When we sat down, he spoke to me about what the job would entail and he more or less told me that if it worked for me, it would work for them too. He was happy to match what I was on in TransferMate. Apart from working in sales, he told me how he would be keen for me to get involved in their sports output, particularly if Kilkenny were to get on a bit of a run this year, something which would supplement my basic salary. He gave me the weekend to think it all over.

I spoke to Anne and we both felt it would be a good opportunity for me to be based solely in Kilkenny work-wise and my profile would suit the job from their point of view. John and I spoke again last Monday and I agreed to take the job.

I had been doing the odd update for *KCLR* on local club matches over the past year or two and have been on air for them various times over the years but I don't think that really had any bearing on my getting the job. Did my hurling career help? Absolutely.

As I've said, the longer you're retired, the less relevant your sporting exploits become but hurling will probably always open some doors for me, like it did with TransferMate, but you have to be able to seize the opportunity when it comes along. TransferMate or *KCLR* wouldn't indulge me because I used to put the ball over the bar for Kilkenny if I wasn't fit to do the job that they had employed me to do and I have a three-month probation period to see out first.

The TransferMate experience ended a lot sooner than I might have expected but it probably paved the way for me to get a job like this as it introduced me to sales for the first time. This new job is just a slightly better fit in that it's all local and would be better suited to me as someone who's well known in the area compared to trying to deal with a complete stranger in America, for example. There'd be no more long drives to different corners of the country either.

I've a lot to be grateful to TransferMate for. Working there helped restore the balance in my life and effectively elongated my club hurling career because something was going to have to give with how the shifts in Pfizer were affecting me. They were very good about my departure too. I had to go and tell my team leader, Karen Brennan, and she was grand about it. They've quite a big operation up there so it's not like I was leaving them in the lurch. 'It's right up your street,' Karen said when I told her that I'd be joining *KCLR* last Tuesday morning. She was happy enough to let me finish up that day as I owed them a week's notice but also had a few days' annual leave still to use up.

I went up to *KCLR* that afternoon and my new manager Marie Smyth was going through the job with me along with John Purcell when she asked, 'When can you start?' 'Tomorrow if you want,' I told her. So I started there last Wednesday morning. I'll be replacing Shane Farrell, *KCLR*'s outgoing sales and marketing executive, who is working out his last couple of weeks there.

That's particularly useful as it gives me the opportunity to shadow him. The job involves going around to businesses to try and get advertisements from them, though most of the clients already have a well-established relationship with the station so it's a maintenance job in some ways. I'd obviously be looking to strengthen those partnerships and bring in extra revenue too. Basically, I'll have a target each month that I'll have to meet.

Shane has been introducing me to clients that I'll be dealing with over the past few days. Already I've met a good few people that I know, like Dermot Grogan, who was corner-back on the James Stephens All-Ireland winning team in 2005, in Grogan and Brown Artisan Butchers, which he part-owns.

I'm really excited by the opportunity. Anne is delighted too and feels that it's the best of both worlds for me. The sales aspect will be the bread and butter of the job but I'm particularly looking forward to getting my teeth into the sports side of it too because it's always been such a huge part of my life. Now I can combine it with my work.

Friday, March 8, 2019

It's birthday week in our house. Mark's on Tuesday and Anne's today. Mark has just turned 14 and he's at that stage where he doesn't want any great fuss over his birthday anymore. Anne looks after all the presents and stuff like that and I think he got some sort of PlayStation game.

He got plenty of cards from his aunts and grandparents too though he's probably more interested in what's in the cards! He doesn't play hurling but he's into soccer and plays with Callan United. He's not too bad at all, I have to say. The work rate could be a little higher – something I like to tell Anne that he takes from her!

There wasn't too much commotion over Anne's birthday either. I just brought home a cake this evening and stuck a candle in it. We hope to get away for a weekend some time soon. Things moved so quickly for us as a couple when we were younger that our birthdays have never been a big deal and it's just as well because I wouldn't be the most thoughtful when it comes to that sort of thing. She drops hints from time to time when we'd be watching television, 'Oh I'd love that' but I'd have it forgotten about as soon as she'd say it. But, in fairness to Anne, she's fairly easy-going that way.

Ellie's birthday is in August and Holly's was last month, February 3. We had a cake for her in the house that day and then we rented a room a couple of weeks later in John Lockes GAA Club in Callan. She hung out there with around 10 of her friends before we had a bit of a party back in the house for her. She plays camogie, volleyball and even Gaelic football, though that's unlikely to last too long around here! The years fly by. It's hard to believe she's 13 now, in first year, going to discos and, of course, developing a bit of an attitude!

A little bit like my own parents though, Anne and I didn't always run in straight lines.

Initially, my relationship with Anne McGeeney was like that between many teenage couples. We got together, we broke up, we fell back in with each other, and so on. I first saw her in The Venue nightclub in Kilkenny when I was about

16, armed with my fake ID. She was easy-going and just generally sound. Funnily enough, I hadn't known her from around town at all. I wouldn't be one for getting too philosophical about it, or anything else for that matter, but we just seemed to get on well and while we frequently went our separate ways, there was a magnetism that always seemed to draw us back together. Chemistry, or whatever.

We continued on this boom and bust cycle for a couple of years, sometimes with a longer hiatus than others. The longer it was, the greater the vacuum and so it happened during one of our lapses that Anne starting seeing someone else, unbeknownst to me initially.

One day I was doing a bit of labouring in what is now The Field bar when I saw Anne walking by the window. I fired her a text. And off it went again, exchanging texts until it came to a head with her telling me that she was pregnant. She had met a guy from Dublin who had been down in Kilkenny one weekend. They kept in touch and had continued to see each other but it was still very early stages for them.

For a lot of lads, that would be an exit-stage-left moment, but that never actually occurred to me. In fairness, when you're a teenager you don't tend to want anything too serious but now it was stick or twist.

I was just gone 20. I concluded that I didn't want to be with anyone else. I wanted to make a proper go of it with Anne this time, even if she was carrying another man's child. So that's what we did.

It wasn't met with universal approval. My mother was ok with it when I explained it to her, but my father certainly wasn't. 'What the fuck are you doing?' he shrieked. Unfortunately, him and Anne didn't get on for a long time but thankfully it's come full circle now and they have a great relationship.

For most of Anne's pregnancy I was undergoing my training in the Defence Forces. With everything that was going on, it'd make you grow up fairly fast. James Stephens were on the way to county, provincial and All-Ireland glory at the time too, while I was going to be joining the Kilkenny panel after that, so I had plenty to keep me distracted. I was living in the barracks during the week and Anne had got an apartment, where I used to spend a lot of my weekends.

When Mark was born on March 5, 2005, I was in the barracks. I popped up the next evening with a bunch of flowers but then a few of her friends came in so I made myself scarce. At that stage, it wasn't quite out there that Anne and I were back on. She had enough to be dealing with so we kept it under wraps for a while. We just went on from there and eventually got our own place together and, while we've had our moments, we haven't looked back. Of course, it's not an ideal scenario to find yourself in but, once it happened, things worked out as well as we could have hoped for.

My own experience growing up in a household without my father stood to me. Paddy had always been very fair to me and I'd like to think I've been the same with Mark. When Anne and I had two girls of our own, they were treated just the same as Mark. He's a great lad and to be fair to him, not once has he ever thrown the 'you're not my father' line at me like I did to Paddy, and he would have had opportunities to do so on occasions.

Thankfully, Mark's father, Warren, is very good to him and we all co-exist with no friction. There were times when things were difficult with my father being resentful towards Paddy and I was caught in the middle. I didn't want that for Mark and thankfully that's never been the case. Warren has Mark up in Dublin regularly and drops him back down, comes in for a cup of coffee and everything's fine. Warren's parents are very good to our other two girls and send presents down, not only to Mark, but to them too.

It was a big shock for us both, to put it mildly, when a couple of months after Mark was born, Anne fell pregnant again, particularly for her. 'I shouldn't be pregnant this soon after having a baby,' she said. Then, like anything, you just get on with it. Financially it was tough, especially as Anne wasn't working at the time, but shortly after Holly was born we moved in with Anne's parents to help us save for a house and they were a great support in many different ways.

My mother was delighted at the thought of having a grandchild, my father less so given the circumstances.

'Are you fucking serious?' he howled.

'Yeah.'

'Are you fucking stupid or something?'

In time, like everything else, he came round of course. I don't actually know how Anne's parents took it as I wasn't around when she told them but there have never been any issues between them and me, to be fair, or indeed with her brother and two sisters.

I had more of a hands-on role than I had with the first pregnancy as we were living together full-time by then, having rented a house on Hawthorn Avenue. Dunnes Stores was open 24 hours a day at the time and many's the time I had to dip in to buy lemon meringue pies – Anne's favourite indulgence to satisfy the cravings that she had at the time. I wasn't present for the labour when Mark was born, but I was with Holly. It started when we were in her parents' house and when I dropped her to the hospital, the doctor told me that she was only in the very early stages and was some way off giving birth. So I went home and picked up the various bits and pieces for Anne and was taking my time about it but when I got back to the hospital the nurse grabbed me and dragged me in. End game was approaching.

I didn't envisage being there, to be honest, and the whole spectacle frightened the life out of me. I was too shy to say, 'Listen, I'm out of here'. In fact, I was too shy to say anything. There wasn't a peep out of me. I was in shock. Anne had an epidural so she wasn't too bad but when it's finally all over it's pretty surreal. Anne was particularly delighted to have a daughter this time but, most importantly, she was healthy.

I was still just 21 and had two children on my hands, though you don't get too bogged down by that sort of stuff for long as there's simply too much to be doing. It was mayhem all the same. Holly was born on a Friday and we had the All-Ireland club semi-final against Portumna two days later, which we lost. I didn't even get to bring them home from the hospital because I was in Thurles.

We tried to take turns with the night feeds but best laid plans and all that. It could be my turn to wake up but Anne would instead, and vice versa, and then Holly never really slept when she was born so the two of us were in a zombie-like state for a long time. In fairness to Mark, he settled after about six weeks and would sleep through the night but Holly was 16 months old before she reached that stage. Later on,

Ellie was a quiet baby, thankfully. We had learned a lot from Holly, however. We'd often let my mother take Holly up when she was asleep but with Ellie, once she was down, she stayed down. My mother and Paddy were very good in lightening our load over that time.

It wasn't easy for Anne rearing young kids when I was playing with Kilkenny and I suppose I could be selfish at times and disappear for a day or two after a championship match. 'The rest of the lads don't have kids at home,' she'd scold me. I just wanted to go out and didn't appreciate that I was leaving her with two children under two years of age. So sometimes I'd just stay in but I'd be as thick as a bull over it. Still, we'd get over it and it wasn't anything that was going to derail us.

We've contemplated having another child but it's highly unlikely to happen at this stage. At this remove, there's a lot to be said for being as far down the road with our children as we are while we're still young ourselves. Yes, it was extremely difficult at times when we were in our early 20s but, now, I'm delighted at how it all worked out. Some of my friends are only having children now and they're doing the night feeds, cleaning bottles, changing nappies and all that, while getting very little sleep. We can all go out and get something to eat in a restaurant as a family now and there's no mayhem attached anymore. Ellie's seven now and just potters away herself. She'll be independent before we're 50.

Mark and Holly are very close in age with just 11 months between them and they're very different characters though they get on very well by and large, while having the rows that all teenagers will have. They'd often go out on the green and have a puckaround but when they go to the same discos they'd move in different circles.

Holly going to discos unnerves me because she's at that age now and I try not to think too much about it. I roll my eyes when I see her all dolled up for these nights out. I wouldn't be bothered about Mark at all because, like any father, you feel that the lads will always be able to look after themselves whereas you fear that the girls are more vulnerable. But, on the other hand, she has a strong personality like her mother and I'm sure she'll be able to look after herself.

Friday, March 15, 2019

I always take the Tuesday and Friday of Cheltenham week off work. Tuesday because, well, it's the first day and then Friday is Gold Cup day. I'm not a big betting man, I wouldn't throw on much more than a few fivers and tenners, and I haven't had many big winners over the years. One year, when Hurricane Fly was at his peak, I had a €500 windfall after backing him to win the Champion Hurdle along with two Irish 'bankers' in other races. I threw on €100, more than I ever would, but I'd never do it again: I was a nervous wreck when the last horse was running!

Cheltenham week is a tradition with a group of my friends. I used to go to the Leopardstown festival over Christmas but not in recent years. The Galway Races usually cut right across the hurling but I went down there a couple of times, including the day after we beat Limerick in the quarter-final in 2012. I remember running into Donal O'Grady, Gavin O'Mahony and a few of the Limerick lads in the Hole in the Wall and having a bit of craic with them. I don't do it for the love of racing and my knowledge of it would be fairly limited.

Outside of the odd horse, I wouldn't place many bets at all, on any sport. It's more for the craic. We always go to The Village Inn this week. There was a huge crowd in the place. My only winner all week was actually one I backed in Dundalk today, Ty Rock Brandy, who came in at 5/1.

When I was playing with Kilkenny it'd be Lucozade only for me on days like this but I can cut loose now and have a few. I obviously have my friends from my hurling background but also from when I played soccer with Ormonde Villa when I was a teenager. James Holden, Mark Wall, Clive Moriarty, Davy Morris, David Carroll, Damien Knox and Eddie Culleton. They wouldn't be that big into hurling though and would struggle to understand why I wouldn't be out on the sessions with them over the years but binging just wasn't an option when playing inter-county hurling. After a few drinks some of them often used to say, 'We just thought you didn't want to come out with us.' They couldn't have been more wrong!

I don't have an addictive personality so gambling was never likely to cause me any great problems but it has become something of an epidemic over the past 10 years or so, particularly given how accessible it is through our smart phones. A few high profile inter-county players have told of the extreme difficulty they were landed in due to gambling. I'd imagine every panel in the country has encountered it to some degree. Were we immune to it in Kilkenny? No, we weren't but, at the same time, I wouldn't say it affected the team. If anyone needed help, it didn't contaminate the dressing room.

I believe the gambling problems that are increasingly prevalent among inter-county players are rooted in the boredom that they experience given that they have no great social outlet over the course of the season. They work, they train, they play. A small handful of our lads developed a habit of going into a casino on Friday nights after training. If we were on a training camp in Carton House, some might nip into Maynooth during our downtime to place a few bets. They wouldn't be putting on loose change.

'What do you do if you lose a few hundred?' I asked one of them one day.

'Always chase your money,' he said, 'you'll always get it back.'

We all laughed at him. We thought it was great sport. But it wasn't. We should have been more compassionate and supportive. I cringe when I think back on that now.

Sunday, March 17, 2019

I can't stand O'Loughlin Gaels. Even at that, I'm being diplomatic. It's customary in the GAA that your nearest rivals are the ones you have the least fondness for, but we have none whatsoever for them. No victory tastes sweeter than when it's against them, while no defeat cuts deeper than when they're inflicting it.

As we see it, they're mouthy off the field and filthy on it. They're not all like that, in fairness. Brian Hogan just wanted to hurl and is one of my best friends from my Kilkenny days. Brian Dowling's a great lad too, along with one or two more. They have some others that I can take or leave but, as a collective, they really boil my piss. Now, they wouldn't exactly be tossing garlands in our direction either.

When they won their first county title in 2001, we were going through a lengthy drought without one and there was a real nouveau riche vibe about them. Then they won it again in 2003 and they enjoyed rubbing our noses in it throughout that period. We could be in the pub and one particular gobshite from O'Loughlins would take special glee in jangling his coins before saying, 'What's that in me pocket, is it change or a county medal?'

There wasn't much I could say at the time but it soon stopped after we won the next two county titles with the small matter of an All-Ireland, which continues to elude them, in between. One of my more memorable St Patrick's Days was in 2011, roaring on Clarinbridge with the lads in The Village Inn as they got a trimming in the club final.

So, here we were this morning, on St Patrick's Day, playing our first competitive game of the year against them in our place on the Kells Road. It's a relatively meaningless competition that's run off for clubs while they don't have access to county players. Enough to take the edge off this game, perhaps? Not at all. My father dreads these games. 'Oh Jesus, I don't know if I can go that,' he says regularly when he finds out we're playing them. He came along this time all the same, as he invariably does.

162

The game was supposed to throw-in as early as 10.30am with the day that was in it, but the referee didn't show up. As 11 o'clock approached, we decided to just get on with it and allowed one of their lads to ref the game until the appointed referee turned up. He never did. The recipe for mayhem was complete. As I saw it, they started acting the prick as the game wore on and one of their defenders was the catalyst for three brawls that broke out. He was slashing at and pulling on lads and then when the row would get going, he'd be nowhere to be seen. Still, Jackie got him with a good belt.

I was involved in the first melee and the third one and ended up with a split fingernail and scratches across my face having had my helmet pulled off. Later, Anne was afraid that she'd be painted as the perpetrator! Even Matthew Ruth, who'd never get involved in that sort of thing, was dragged into it and we had good craic with him afterwards. No one was sent off though the 'ref' ordered that one of our lads be replaced at one stage. We finished strongly in the end, hitting 1-3 without reply to get a draw. 'I would have just sent them on their merry way and just had a training session,' said my father afterwards. 'I wouldn't have even entertained that.'

Ellie was taking part in the parade in Kilkenny this afternoon then with her dance class. I walked behind them along with a number of parents in case any of them got nervous but they carried off their little routine in front of the reviewing stand without a hitch.

With the parade at 1.30pm, it meant that I missed the All-Ireland club final as Ballyhale Shamrocks swept St Thomas's aside. It could hardly be further removed from the nothing league game that we played this morning.

I don't torment myself every St Patrick's Day about not being in Croke Park with the club but, since 2005, March 17 has certainly been anticlimactic.

James Stephens' All-Ireland club title win sits at the very top of my hurling achievements with club or county. I won my eight All-Irelands with Kilkenny after it, but none of them surpassed that. It's a much harder medal to win. You're not playing with the cream of the county. It's your corner of Kilkenny coming out on top against all of the other corners of all of the other counties in Ireland. Like any youngster, I grew up dreaming of winning All-Irelands with Kilkenny. I saw it happen in front of my own eyes. I knew that if I ever got a run with the county team, there was a more than reasonable chance that I'd win an All-Ireland.

With the club, it was different. Until 2004, when I was playing, I had never even seen James Stephens win a county title. So the idea of going all the way to Croke Park with The Village never entered my head. It was a pipe dream. But when we won that elusive county title, the confidence we took from it carried us. We felt like we could do anything after it. We rode our luck a little in the Leinster final against UCD but we beat O'Donovan Rossa comfortably in the All-Ireland semi-final to set up a meeting with Athenry.

They were far more experienced in this business than us, having won three titles since 1997 and still retained players like Joe Rabbitte and Eugene Cloonan and other current and former Galway players; Philly Larkin and Brian McEvoy weren't long finished with Kilkenny and Peter Barry was still there. Jackie, Eoin McCormack and myself were coming through. We won by five points and I was named man of the match after hitting 0-9.

Although I hadn't yet experienced an All-Ireland with Kilkenny at that stage, it's completely different. There was no 82,000 in Croke Park, wearing suits for the banquet in the Citywest later that evening and a homecoming in front of thousands the following night. It was on the bus and straight back to the club that evening to celebrate among your own.

We made sure the bus went down John Street, an O'Loughlin's stronghold. A couple of our lads were hanging out of the coach and we were all banging the windows. There were lads diving off the street and into the pubs to avoid the spectacle.

When we got to the club, the crowd waiting to greet us was phenomenal. We couldn't even get into the place. It was so difficult to get to the bar that some of the lads had to go to an off-licence to buy drink and sit out the front of the clubhouse while they had it. I remember getting a picture with my father and Seamus Delaney, a local publican, and beyond leaving at 6.30am I don't recall a whole lot more.

Within 10 days I had made my senior debut for Kilkenny against Dublin at Parnell Park and we went on to win the National League. Things ultimately didn't work out in the championship for Kilkenny that year but we rolled back into another county final with the club, beating Ballyhale Shamrocks, and retained the Leinster title too. Then we faced an emerging Portumna side in the All-Ireland semi-final and they beat us well.

Philly had struggled with his back that year and Anne had only given birth to Holly two days before, while we also suffered a red card, things we couldn't afford against a formidable team en route to the first of their four titles.

Afterwards we were drowning our sorrows in Delaney's when Brian McEvoy piped up. 'What are ye all down in the dumps for? There's three-in-a-row to go for here!' And when we reflected on it, we appreciated how much of a good run we had been on, winning two counties, a couple of Leinsters and an All-Ireland. With the team we had, I expected more to come but there's only been one county title since, in 2011, and we weren't properly prepared for the Leinster campaign that year after beating Ballyhale in a replay. I still wonder where we could have gone if we had more time before playing Oulart-The Ballagh and if Jackie hadn't been suspended.

It's probably the biggest regret of my career that the club hasn't got back to Croke Park. The chances are dwindling for me now, but I certainly haven't given up hope yet.

Winning the All-Ireland club title with Ballyhale Shamrocks is a huge achievement for Henry Shefflin in his first season as a manager. They had 10 players aged 21 or younger and three of them still in St Kieran's College. It's unheard of, really. Once they got out of Kilkenny, nobody laid a glove on them.

Another emerging Ballyhale team certainly isn't encouraging for everyone else in Kilkenny. We were the last team to beat them in a knockout tie, the 2017 county semi-final, and it emerged after today's game that Henry referenced it in the dressing room at half-time. They held a similar lead at the midway point that day as they had today but we blew them away in the second half. Look where they've gone since compared to us.

Unsurprisingly, Henry is now being touted as Brian Cody's eventual successor. I could see it happening and yet, at the same time, I couldn't. If Brian was to step aside in the near future, Henry would probably be a shoo-in but I don't expect that he will. And who knows what the lay of the land will be when that time comes around? The timing may not be right for Henry; he's not that long gone from Kilkenny and went straight from playing with his club to managing them. He's got a young family and it's a massive commitment. Maybe there'll be others with strong credentials too by the time the vacancy arises.

What I could see happening is Brian bringing Henry in as a selector or coach before eventually being succeeded by him. I say that partly because he would have privately sought his opinion on various matters over the years in a way that he wouldn't have with other players. I'm not saying that Brian would have acted on everything that Henry suggested, but he certainly would have taken it on board. The pair of them worked very well together and weren't Kilkenny lucky that their playing and managerial careers intersected.

I'd imagine they'd be rather different as managers purely because they're very different people. Henry would be more personable and would get involved in a bit of a sneer or the craic, whereas Cody wouldn't. Then again, maybe he did when he was 30 years younger and only distanced himself from that once he became manager. I really don't know.

However, I would think that the two of them would be similar in terms of the culture that they'd build around the set up and the values that they would demand from their players. If Henry were to be the next Kilkenny manager, the transition would be pretty seamless in that regard, I'd imagine.

We've seen in various sports how managers who succeed iconic long-serving figures often struggle. Manchester United is an obvious example but Henry Shefflin succeeding Brian Cody would be rather different to Wilf McGuinness or David Moyes slotting in after Matt Busby or Alex Ferguson. He'd instantly command the same respect as Cody without having to lift a finger given what he's done in the game.

Henry is the best that I have ever played with. Was he the most skilful? Not quite; others like Tommy Walsh and Richie Power and DJ Carey had a greater array in that respect. The likes of DJ and Eddie Brennan would have had more pace than Henry. But when you add everything up, there was no one better than him. It was his willingness to work so hard that made him the greatest. Brian would have always pointed out to us how Henry does the extra things, how he's out on the training pitch before everyone and last off it. He had a path worn around the field out the back of his house from pounding it.

Would I have eight All-Ireland medals only for Henry Shefflin? Absolutely not. Would I have won any without him? Probably, but you still couldn't be sure. I'd seriously doubt whether we could have stopped Cork in 2006 if we didn't have Henry. We had a lot of inexperienced players at the time, none more so than myself. And then if we don't win that, they're on three-in-a-row, going for four. Brian could have been coming under pressure. Do we win the All-Ireland in 2007 as comfortably then without the confidence of winning the year before? Do we reach the pinnacle of 2008? The three subsequent finals against Tipperary? Of course, the collective always trumped any individual with us but Henry opened more doors for us than anyone else.

You always knew when playing with him that if you made a good run and it was the right ball, you'd get it off him. With other players you might check your run to make sure they'd see you or allow for the likelihood of them miscontrolling the ball, though never with Henry.

I remember in the 2006 league final against Limerick, for example, I was moving up the field, not necessarily looking for a pass, when he pinged it between a few defenders – real eye-of-the-needle stuff – into my path. I didn't have to break stride and scored a goal from there. Nobody else would have tried it, never mind execute it. His presence on the field would give you that extra bit of confidence. That if we needed a lift, he could always provide it.

The drawn All-Ireland final in 2012 is one of many such instances and a game that Henry identified as his best once he retired. So many of us were sluggish that day and he just galvanised the team. You wanted the ball to go to him every time because he was on such a high. I was captain at the time and actually advised him to take a point with the penalty late on when the sides were level. That's what he did but I'd imagine he would have done it anyway.

That incident became a talking point ahead of the replay after Joe Canning alleged that JJ had expressed his displeasure at Henry's choice down the other end of the field. We didn't believe it but, regardless of whether JJ said that or not, it shouldn't have come out of his mouth, along with saying that Henry was 'not sportsmanlike'. He made it worse then by not owning it once he'd said it. That kind of stuff doesn't happen in Kilkenny and we used that ahead of the replay, big time.

Comparisons have been made between Shefflin and Canning but I just don't see it. Canning would have more about him in terms of raw natural ability but the influence either player has wielded on big games is where the chasm develops. Joe has improved on that front in the last few years but too often over the course of his career he hasn't been a factor for long periods of really big matches, a charge that couldn't be levelled at Henry in all of the years that he played. So any comparison between the two just isn't valid for me.

Centre-forward was probably where Henry was most effective but if you were getting good ball into him at full-forward he was lethal given how strong he was and the eye he had for goal. Did his game have any weaknesses? No obvious ones. You could say his high fielding in a group of players could have been better. Now, don't get me wrong, he still had great hands, particularly when coming from behind you to catch a ball. But he wouldn't be like Tommy or JJ in that respect. He wasn't slow but, again, he didn't have the burst of pace that DJ or Eddie would have had. This is nitpicking, though.

As I've said, his greatest asset was his willingness to work so hard to improve himself, but also on the field during games. It's almost unheard of, across any team sport, for someone so talented to work as hard as he did. That work rate was infectious and was gold dust for Cody as a manager.

Off the field, Henry's always been a very easy chap to get along with, though he wouldn't have socialised with us much after games, save for All-Irelands. I presume he'd have done more of that when he was younger but by the time I came on the scene he was one of the more senior players and he went on to have a family.

He wasn't a loudmouth in the dressing room but he'd say his bit without jumping up and banging the table. He'd speak with a real passion though. On occasions, he shed tears as he spoke to us after battling back from one of his many injuries in the latter years of his career. How he didn't know whether he'd be able to get back. You could see just how much it meant to him.

To be able to come back from all those injuries spoke so much about his willpower. I often said that if I did my cruciate I'd really struggle to jump all the fences required to get back. To do it a second time? That would be even worse because you'd know exactly what you were facing into.

He also had a major shoulder operation and numerous problems with his foot. Every time he came back as good as ever – except for his last year in 2014. He picked up a stress fracture in his foot and couldn't get back in the team during the championship. His sharpness, his speed, it was like it all went at once. You were waiting for it to come back, like it had every time before, but it just didn't happen for him. He still won his record 10th All-Ireland that year and it was a fitting way for him to bow out.

On reflection, you could argue that Henry Shefflin was fortunate to have come along when he did but, for me, the luck was all ours.

Sunday, March 24, 2019

Yesterday was my youngest brother Allen's Confirmation day. He only turned 12 last November and our eldest two actually made their Confirmation before him. I don't remember much about my Confirmation, back in 1997. I got a ball of money but have no idea what I spent it on. I do recall being in my school uniform for the ceremony and being excited that I had 'Confirmation clothes' for afterwards. I think I wore a cardigan and a shirt.

I had Philly Larkin as my sponsor, although he isn't my Godfather. But he's related to me and was hurling for Kilkenny at the time so that granted him enough deity in my world. I am Allen's Godfather though and was his sponsor so I had to accompany him up to the bishop and place my hand on his shoulder as he was confirmed. I must admit, I don't go to Mass all year round or anything like it, but I don't believe you need to do all that to be religious. I do have a faith in God, though.

My mother is away in Cork this weekend for her sister's birthday but otherwise she'd have dropped down to my father's house for the party after the Confirmation Mass where there was food and a few drinks. That's all normalised in my family now. It's similar with Kim, who came up from Cork with all her family and met our Aunt Mary and Uncle Ned, my father's siblings, for the first time and other members of the wider family.

Although we're in regular contact, I don't see Kim as often as I would like but my father has been down to Cork a number of times and there was no question of her not being invited.

She seems very relaxed in our company but I sense that she doesn't want to push the boat out too far either. I didn't get to talk to her much yesterday but she was staying overnight in a hotel and I suggested that she call to us on her way back to Cork today.

'I don't want to put ye out,' she said.

'You're not putting us out, you're family,' Anne told her. 'We want you to see where we live and we want the girls to come up and play with Holly and Ellie.'

Kim's girls are now much more comfortable in the company of ours and they got on very well together yesterday. Allen gelled well with them too. They called today after all but were pretty tired so they didn't stay too long.

It was a profitable weekend for Allen, all told. I saw him this morning before I went to training.

'How much did you get?' I asked him.

'Six-hundred euro, on the button,' he said.

He doesn't know what he'll do with it but I'm sure a chunk of it will be spent on something hurling-related. Given the age difference and the fact that we never really lived together, our relationship isn't typical of most siblings. I was already a father when Allen was born so it was a bit surreal, at 22 years of age, holding my new-born brother in the hospital. Personality-wise, I see more of his mother, Veronica, in him than my father. It's always difficult, looking back, to imagine just what you were like at Allen's age but I think I was pretty different to him. He's mad into hurling like I was though and, of course, it comes full circle: I chide him now about not hitting the ball on his weaker side like Fan Larkin did with me all those years ago.

He's a good little hurler but there's nothing to him physically just yet. As the youngest, his distaste for certain foods is indulged more than mine would have been. I cornered him one day: 'Brian Cody was on to me and he said you're not eating potatoes!' So he started eating them religiously for a couple of weeks, and then he stopped.

Maybe when I'm on the way down and he's on the way up our hurling careers will intersect on a junior team when he's coming into adulthood and I'm tipping 40. If not, I know he'll hurl for the club at least and I look forward to enjoying his career, whatever level he gets to, long after mine is finished.

8

APRIL

'I'd love to get Hurler of the Year.'
'Do you think you can get it?'
'Yeah, I think I could, yeah.'

A stipulation of each five-year contract you sign with the Defence Forces is that you go on a tour of duty over the course of that period. I completed two tours, to Kosovo in 2007 and then Syria, eight years later. The contrast between both experiences and their respective knock-on effects when I came home could hardly have been more stark, however.

I was almost three years in the army by the time the Kosovo trip, a NATO mission, came up. Generally the tours last six months and you can choose to go for the summer or winter. Summer wasn't an option for me with my Kilkenny career so I was looking at an October-April trip. When the Kosovo opportunity arose in 2007, I applied and was successful. I had completed three years on the Kilkenny panel at that stage but wasn't so comfortable that I could make any assumptions about my spot. So I called Brian Cody.

'Will I be involved when I get back?' I wondered.

'Do you want to be involved?'

'Of course I do, yeah.'

'Well then you'll be involved.'

When you're in the Irish army, tours of duty are relatively lucrative. Our wages weren't great but when on overseas trips you get your wage at home and another for your tour of duty, so you're essentially doubling your money. At the time, Anne and I were trying to get a deposit together for a house. We were living with Anne's parents and saving every cent we had so we didn't have any great outgoings and I spent very little while in Kosovo.

Naturally, having lived all my life in Kilkenny, it was an experience I looked forward to. I was 23 at the time. Other people my age were going away to Australia for a year or two, something that wasn't on my radar. But it would have been worrying for my family. Although the worst of the conflict had passed in Kosovo, you're still going away to a war-torn country and, while it's very rarely happened, Irish soldiers have been killed on these type of missions in the past.

There were 200 troops in the camp over there. I actually left a few days later than the rest as I had a county semi-final for James Stephens against Ballyhale Shamrocks four days after the scheduled departure date.

I flew out the next morning after we lost but was back within two weeks to play for the Defence Forces in a game against An Garda Síochána in Croke Park and actually attended the county final. Times have changed. You don't get leeway like that anymore.

By then, the focus in Kosovo was just on rebuilding after years of war but riots would still break out occasionally. We were busy out there but never in any danger. There was always something to do. There were the normal duties in the camp and we did a lot of checkpoints and patrols, checking for weapons, which got the locals' backs up as they went about their daily business. There would have been a certain amount of resentment towards us over there for that.

There was a social outlet. We'd have a few beers in the canteen at night from time to time and every few weeks we'd get a minibus down to a Swedish camp where there'd be a rock band playing. I even made it on TV while I was out there as Richard Corrigan, the chef, was shooting a show and some of us were giving him a hand with a barbecue. I was snapped for the *Irish Independent* another day, holding my rifle at a checkpoint. It was tough being out there at Christmas but I came home a couple of days after it and flew straight out on the Kilkenny team holiday to Thailand and Dubai. I also got home for Peter Cleere's wedding that November. You were allowed a few weeks leave and I took mine in two blocks, though now you have to take it all in one.

Much of my downtime in Kosovo was dedicated towards my fitness. I was still very insecure about my place in the Kilkenny set up and feared losing too much ground while over there that I wouldn't be able to make up. I was in touch with Mick Dempsey on a regular basis about what runs and gym work I ought to have been doing. I'd talk to him on the phone the odd time though mostly we communicated through text or email. I was very disciplined. I had three tracks that I listened to almost on a loop when out running or in the gym – that Al Pacino speech from 'Any Given Sunday', the Survivor classic 'Eye of the Tiger' and Tina Turner's 'Simply The Best'. I admit that I wouldn't be getting any extra marks for originality on that score but they worked for me.

At one stage I hurt my Achilles, probably because I was overdoing it. No matter. I just jumped on the spinning bike and pedalled furiously for an hour at a time until I could run again. It was only in the last three weeks or so that I took out the hurl and ball. I reasoned I wouldn't be any sharper than if I'd done it for the six months I was out there. I was always going to be behind in that respect no matter what I did.

When I got home in April 2008 I realised that, physically, I was in the shape of my life. Anne and my mother commented on my appearance straight away. 'Jaysus, there's not a pick on you!' I wasn't the most natural athlete but here I was leading out the runs with Kilkenny. That hadn't happened before. My touch obviously wasn't up to scratch but I soon caught up.

A few weeks after I returned to training, there were pre-championship debriefs with the management and the players on an individual basis. I was asked what my ambition was for the year.

'Well, I want to get on the panel first, then try and get on the team after that.'

Martin Fogarty cornered me.

'Yeah, but what's your ambition?' he wondered.

'I'd love to get Hurler of the Year.'

'Do you think you can get it?'

'Yeah, I think I could, yeah.'

In truth, it wasn't something that just popped into my head there and then. I carried that ambition to Kosovo with me and it framed everything that I did out there. It was rooted in my insecurity within the Kilkenny team and panel. Before every team announcement I'd be tormented that I wouldn't be picked. 'This is it now, I won't be playing.' I'd have Anne and my parents gone mad.

But while those fears were generally misplaced once I broke into the team, my confidence wasn't helped by the fact that I was regularly taken off in games, with the 2007 All-Ireland final a welcome exception. I was three years on the team coming into 2008 and I needed to shake off that negative mindset if I was to fulfil my potential. So I set myself the ultimate goal – to be Hurler of the Year. This was something that I felt I could achieve if I applied myself properly and toughened up mentally.

I was just home and wasn't playing when Kilkenny lost the league semi-final to Tipperary in Nowlan Park so all that was in front of me was the championship. It meant that I only played four games for Kilkenny that year, against Offaly, Wexford, Cork and Waterford. My form was excellent; I helped myself to a goal in both the All-Ireland semi-final and final as we stormed to the three-in-a-row.

As is the tradition, the All-Ireland winning manager announces the Hurler of the Year on All Star night. I was nominated along with Waterford's Eoin Kelly and Eddie Brennan. I could see a small smile roll across Brian Cody's lips as he announced the winner and betrayed a little bit of club bias while he was at it. 'The Hurler of the Year is from Kilkenny, James Stephens' Eoin Larkin.'

It was unbelievably satisfying to have set myself such a lofty goal and to have achieved it, particularly in a year when that Kilkenny team was at what proved to be its peak. As well as being named Hurler of the Year, I also picked up the Texaco and GPA awards for good measure, along with my first All Star.

Martin Fogarty approached me later that night. 'Fair play to you,' he said. 'You said you wanted to get Hurler of the Year and you went off and got it.' A text came in from my father. 'My heart is bursting out of my chest.' Anne was with me but she was too busy running around looking for Kieran Donaghy for a photograph!

How much would I put what I did that year down to the fact that I was in Kosovo for six months? All of it, to be honest. It played a trick on me mentally. When I left I was worried that I wouldn't push myself as hard in training as I would if Mick Dempsey and Brian Cody were looking on. As it turned out, that drove me even harder. Moreover, there was no chipper down the road to tempt me. No chocolate in the fridge. No domestic distractions. I had little going on in Kosovo outside of my duties and training. That all helped, big time. As a life experience it was fantastic too, working in an environment like that, even if some awful atrocities provided the backdrop to it all.

None of the accolades from my hurling career adorn our home in Callan – Anne doesn't want 'dust-gatherers' around the place – and most of them are in my old bedroom in my mother's house. If I had to choose out of all of them though, the Hurler of the Year trophy would be the one. Whenever I hear any of those three tracks that I had on my iPod while pounding the roads or pumping weights in the gym in Kosovo, that nice warm glow of satisfaction from 2008 washes all over me again.

Unfortunately, I never played quite as well over a season after that, though I had a fine year in 2009, winning another All Star. I was man of the match in a cracking Leinster semi-final in Tullamore against Galway, who threw everything at us in their first year in the province. I finished the All-Ireland final against Tipperary very strongly that year too. So it would be wrong to say that the weight of Hurler of the Year knocked me off my stride or was a burden to carry, as Austin Gleeson intimated after he won it in 2016. I just got on with it.

I had my dips and bad games like every player has but, by and large, my form was pretty good for a number of years after 2008 without getting as close to that level of performance as I would have liked. I don't really know why that was but I guess I had a lot going on with work and rearing a family and probably just didn't have the mental space to find that zone again.

So, when another tour of duty came up in late 2015, I thought this could be an opportunity to get back to absolute peak form again, even if I was 31 by then. I couldn't have been more wrong. If I played my best hurling after going to Kosovo, my career and, more to the point, my life, hit rock bottom on the back of the trip to Syria.

The Road to Damascus may have seen the conversion of Saint Paul a couple of thousand years ago, but my experience of it wasn't quite as profound. It was just part of a completely dispiriting ordeal that was my second tour of duty. As each week passed, another layer of resilience was stripped off me.

It needn't have been like this. On the surface, it should have been another great trip and I was fortunate in the job I had as I was simply required to drive the deputy force commander around. It involved frequent trips to Damascus, which was only about a 45-minute drive if you could go directly from Camp Zouaini in Golan Heights, but the Israelis' border control meant that we couldn't go that route. So it became an eight-hour drive instead.

It was a handy number for me, avoiding the more run-of-the-mill tasks back at the camp and cruising around in a swanky Mitsubishi Pajero, staying in a fine hotel in Damascus or Tel Aviv or Jerusalem with lovely food and a state of the art gym, the like of which I would have smashed eight years earlier. But I just didn't want to do it. The more time went on, I didn't want to do anything.

I remember the first morning coming in the gate of the camp in October 2015 and saying to myself, 'Fucking hell, what am I doing here? I really don't want to be here.' But then I reassured myself. I had similar feelings when arriving in Kosovo years before and that turned out to be a great experience. And, as it turned out, I was grand for the first couple of weeks in Syria. Then, slowly but surely, things just got progressively worse.

We were only there a few weeks when a huge bomb went off in the middle of the night and shook the place. The bed even moved a bit, despite the explosion being a few miles away. I thought I was imagining it. Then, maybe 30 seconds later, another one went off. 'Get in the bunker!' Lads were screaming and running everywhere. You didn't have time to be frightened, you just moved. It turned out that the bombs were scare tactics on the part of ISIS. Nobody was injured though we had an observation post closer to where they went off and the windows were blown out. Some warning shot! It wouldn't exactly lift your spirits.

Look, we weren't in the thick of it and I wouldn't want to overplay it but we were closer than anyone would want to be at the same time. ISIS was taking over and trying to gain as much ground as they could. The previous group from the Kilkenny barracks that had been out there had to flee their camp because the rebels were moving in. We were part of a United Nations Disengaging Observer Force so you're obviously not out there to get involved in combat. We were essentially there to show the locals that there is a presence, so that they're not so on edge.

Driving the deputy force commander around was essentially my entire brief. He was from Dublin, a nice man, and though he didn't have much interest in hurling, he was into rugby and we'd chat away about sport. When on the road, you'd often see nothing but rubble from where the streets in Syria have been blown to shreds. People living in shacks. You'd rarely see children out and about.

I'm not saying that all of this sank my mood, but I wasn't in a good headspace anyway having not confronted my depression properly when it first arose a few years earlier. So being out there certainly wasn't going to lift me out of it, especially being away from my family.

I was lucky enough to get home at Christmas, though I

didn't go on the Kilkenny team holiday this time, the first one I missed over the years. I'd have had no time at home with the kids if I'd gone to Jamaica and New York with the team. We got vouchers from the county board and planned to go on a family holiday when I got home from Syria in April.

Technology had moved on a bit from when I was in Kosovo and I could FaceTime the family every day while in Syria. That should soften the blow of being away but, in ways, it only made it harder. Ellie, our youngest, had a tough time while I was gone.

She's always been a daddy's girl and was only four at the time. She was wearing a path to the doctor; there always seemed to be some ailment or another and she was missing a lot of school. Anne reckoned it was because I was away. When we'd FaceTime, Ellie would rarely talk to me. She was angry at me for going away, essentially feeling that I'd deserted her. Mark and Holly were older and they were fine but it was tough when Ellie wouldn't say a word to me. It was like that for virtually the whole six months I was away. When I came home at Christmas she was delighted to see me and things were back to normal but as soon as I went back to Syria, it was all picture, no sound again.

I didn't train as hard as I had in Kosovo, but there was at least some sound thinking behind it. I did a good bit of running out there but I was after having a couple of injuries; my hamstring was tight and my shoulder was bothering me along with a few other bits and pieces so I decided I wasn't going to touch any weights. With the running, I was fairly well disciplined before Christmas but when I went back it was much more of a chore. There were good days but more bad ones. On the whole, my mood was continually dropping. I just wanted to be home.

I was on edge while in Damascus too. I'd drop my superior off for a meeting and I'd constantly be checking the wing mirrors to see if fellas were pulling up and not coming back, fearing a car bomb. It was irrational, because Damascus had gone largely untouched in the whole conflict.

It got to a stage where I just wanted to lie on my bed and not do anything beyond watching Netflix. The 12 weeks that I had to put in after Christmas seemed never-ending. I'd moan to Anne how sick of the place I was, that I had to get home.

Eventually, I decided that I was getting out of there. A rumour went around that the tour was to be extended by a week or two and that was the last thing I needed to hear. It wouldn't be unusual in camp for something like that to do the rounds and prove to be utterly false, but once that entered the equation, my conviction that I had to get out of there only hardened. So I went to the commandant and sold him a cock and bull story. I actually told him that there were issues with Anne, that she had depression. Of course, at that stage, I was still in complete denial about my own mental health problems so the irony and hypocrisy of that stunt was completely lost on me. Needless to say, Anne wasn't impressed. 'You can't say that! What if they send someone out?'

Anyway, they bought my story and I managed to get home two weeks early but even that was a slog. The first flight was late so I missed the connecting one in Zürich and had to hang around for the whole day.

Sure enough, as Anne feared, the army did send someone out to us, a personal support officer from the barracks, to see if I needed help with anything given the reasons I had presented for having to come home, though I assured him we were fine.

Initially, I felt like, 'I'm home now, I'll be grand' and then we went on our holiday to Florida a couple of weeks later and had a good time with the kids in Disney World. I was in good form but I was only kicking the can down the road. I went back training with Kilkenny that April. I hadn't done as much work as I had in Kosovo and was now eight years older so I wasn't like the spring lamb that arrived back in 2008. The older you get, the harder you need to train to stay in touch and here I was doing less.

It's a regret that I didn't get so much more out of the trip to Syria as, let's face it, it's unlikely that I'll have the opportunity to work overseas again. Kosovo was a tremendous experience for me on so many levels and had a really positive impact in various ways, not least on my hurling. I should have enjoyed Syria every bit as much, probably even more given the job I was lucky enough to have while out there.

If I had really listened to Anne a few years earlier and confronted my problems I would have been in the right headspace to enjoy it properly. Who knows, if I had embraced everything about it like I had in Kosovo, I might have put myself in a position to enjoy an Indian summer with my hurling career; get right back to the levels I was at in 2008 and maybe even put myself in the running for Hurler of the Year again. But I was only phoning it in as the 2016 championship approached.

####

Wednesday, April 17, 2019

Mayo footballer Lee Keegan was quoted in the media today talking about alcohol bans in inter-county panels. He said they don't have one in Mayo.

'If you want to be playing at the highest level it's really at your discretion and it'll show up if you're not performing that you're not doing your stuff outside of training,' he said.

We didn't have drink bans in Kilkenny as such either. It was largely self-regulated and there weren't too many that stepped out of line. I recall a young chap who came onto the panel one year and he'd have been having a good time while he was away in college during the week. He was cut after a few weeks. You absolutely couldn't afford to burn the candle at both ends when you were trying to break into the Kilkenny panel at that stage.

Over the course of the inter-county season, my drinking would be very limited. During the league, as a team, we'd go out very little. If there was a bit of a gap between games we might go out and have a few pints and then after the final, if we got that far, you could have that night and the day after. The same after championship matches, and we'd enjoy those couple of days, but in a lot of years we only played four games. So you're talking about maybe five or six sessions a year from the start of the league to the end of the championship.

I generally wouldn't even drink after club games that we'd have in between county matches. If Anne and I went out for a meal there'd be no alcohol involved on my end. I was best man at my friend James Holden's wedding one year. Didn't touch a drop. There were very occasional breaches of discipline over the years but they'd be dealt with swiftly and quietly, to the extent that there was an incident before an All-Ireland final one year that I didn't hear about for weeks afterwards.

Once the inter-county season was over, there would invariably be a number of club games and between those and other things you'd cram in quite a lot of socialising from there to Christmas until you have to resume Kilkenny training. Then it's back on the dry again.

I just saw the curtailment of my social life as something I had to do if I wanted to be an inter-county hurler. I missed plenty of weddings and stag weekends and while I wouldn't say it was difficult, there would be pangs of regret when the lads are heading off and you're getting your gear ready to go training that Friday night. But nothing more than that.

People draw comparisons between professional rugby players and inter-county hurlers and footballers, as Lee Keegan did, but I don't think it's valid. 'I always look at professional sports and particularly rugby; they have their few beers after their game and they train two days later and perform at the highest level the week after,' he said. But it's a completely different dynamic for them. I'd imagine that they have pretty intensive pre-season training and don't drink at all during that period while having everything laid on for them.

For GAA players, they have work and have to look after all their own meals and nutrition. They're training in the evening after their day's work, while the rugby players' day's work is the training itself that morning. And if they go drinking after a game, they have ample time and facilities to get their recovery in and they're not putting down a week's work, in the conventional sense at least, like a GAA player does before the next game. That all counts in a big way.

So while some may feel that it's too stringent for amateur players, I think that the balance that is there at the moment for inter-county players in terms of their social activity is pretty much bang on. If you want to play at the highest level and really get the best out of yourself, this is what you have to do, in my opinion. Drinking every weekend, or even every couple of weekends, has no place in that. There are still the few opportunities during the year to blow off steam and plenty more once the season is over and, indeed, once you finish playing altogether.

I'm conscious of the fact that I was fortunate enough to be born in a perennially successful county when saying this, but there's no compulsion to commit to an inter-county panel so you might as well do it right once you do.

####

Wednesday, April 24, 2019

I could easily have quit hurling after last Saturday. Mullinavat beat us in our second league game after we had already lost to Bennettsbridge. The league is directly linked to the championship in Kilkenny so these aren't meaningless matches. I didn't even go out after the game on Saturday.

There was an '80s and '90s disco in the club that I was supposed to go to but I just couldn't face it. I was afraid of what I might say to one of the lads on the team if I had a few drinks in me. The same failings as last year, and previous years, are still apparent and it's incredibly frustrating. Anne knew I was like a dog over it.

'When are you training again?'

'I don't know.'

She'd be laughing at the good of it but I was just so hurt over the whole thing. If no one let me know when training was on again I wouldn't have bothered my arse finding out. But sure enough, it pops up on the WhatsApp group so I gathered my gear and went out the door last night. What infuriates me most is that we're capable of so much more. The talent is there.

The challenge matches in the run-up to the Bennettsbridge game had been going well. But when the pressure comes on in real games, we struggle to deal with it. I wasn't exactly burning it up myself either. I was wing-forward for most of both games and just wasn't involved either day. My hip and groin problems had flared up again and I had a sinus infection last week but, inevitably, you think that maybe this is just the way it goes when you're approaching your 35th birthday, that your powers are waning and you're not one of the club's marquee players anymore. That you're going to become increasingly peripheral until you find yourself on the bench and being phased out, down to the junior team.

I couldn't fault Cheddar, he's been very good. His attention to detail is very impressive. It's probably been a bit of an eye-opener for him; I'd imagine he thought we'd have a better base level of performance than we've turned in so far. He must be wondering what to do next. After the Bennettsbridge match we had some hard sessions and hard words from him too. He spoke to us about the perception that he would have had about The Village going back to his own playing days, that we were hard and that he expected tough men when he came down to us.

'From what I can see, that's not how it is now so we'll just have to become like that,' he said. 'I'm not condoning dirty play or anything like that but I do want it tough and hard.'

Then it was more of the same against Mullinavat. We gave away so many frees which John Walsh just popped over the bar. Silly frees for pulling the jersey and that sort of harmless stuff. We couldn't give away a good free, where you just mow a lad and let him know that if he's coming in here, this is what he's getting. I'd say the Mullinavat lads walked off the field without a mark on them.

I haven't really spoken to Jackie about it. He said a few words at training last night and I did too. 'Here we are again and it's me and Jackie and Mattic doing the talking again. This shouldn't be Cheddar or Séamus driving this, it should be player-led,' I told them. 'The lads lay out the drills and they shouldn't have to say another thing.'

Hopefully the penny will drop. Next up are Ballyhale Shamrocks, the All-Ireland club champions, and then we won't have another game of consequence until August. It'll be a long few months if we don't show something against them.

Tuesday, April 30, 2019

I was listening to *2FM* in the car today and Lottie Ryan was talking about how it was the ninth anniversary of her father

Gerry's death. It was the first time that I realised that he had died on the same day that Anne and I were married.

We covered quite a lot of ground together in our early 20s with Mark and Holly coming along so getting married wasn't quite the milestone for us that it would have been for other couples. We knew we were staying together. But we had a lovely, simple day surrounded by the people that meant most to us.

I'm not one for grand romantic gestures and there was no great spontaneity to the engagement. We had talked about it and by the time it became official, it was just about completing the formalities.

At the time we were saving to buy a house and living with Anne's parents. We had a bit of money set aside at that stage and just dipped into it for the ring, which Anne picked out. We marched straight out of the shop and up to the fountain on the grounds of Kilkenny Castle where I got down on one knee. She said yes, I stood up, we kissed and then back to Anne's parents to break the news.

We got married in Foulkstown Church with just close friends and family present and then we had a reception in Cillin Hill. James Holden was my best man. Mark was page boy and Holly the flower girl. Tommy, Jackie and Brian Dowling were among the Kilkenny hurlers present. A hundred or so more joined us after the meal, including Brian Cody, who gave us a really generous gift.

We got married on a Friday and the National League final was on that weekend, but we weren't in it. In the first 10 seasons I played with Kilkenny, we reached the league final eight times but thankfully 2010 was one of the bogey years so

I could relax and enjoy the whole day, save for the cheesiness of our first dance to Shania Twain's From This Moment On!

There was no honeymoon as such. We just hadn't the time or the money either, I suppose. We did go to New York for a week a couple of years later, just the two of us, which was the unofficial honeymoon.

When we woke up this morning Anne greeted me with 'happy anniversary'. 'I remember it like it was yesterday,' I say to her every year, 'and if it was tomorrow I wouldn't go!' I put in a request on John Walsh's breakfast show on *KCLR* for her: 'Happy ninth anniversary Anne Larkin, from Eoin.' Perks of the job, I guess, though she didn't even hear it. We sat down this evening after I got in from training and just watched television together, like any other day, no frills.

But next year will be our tenth anniversary and we're talking about going on a cruise.

####

The highlight of my wedding anniversary was getting into a fight in training actually. I was chasing down Jack McGrath, who has a slightly unorthodox striking action. It's just a bit unusual how he swings the hurl, which makes him particularly awkward to hook.

As I tried to do so, I caught him on the hand. He still got something of a strike on the ball and off it went but he turned around to me straight away and held the bas of the hurl out while adopting a stance that suggested he was going to jab it into my belly, so I tensed up. Then he seemed to stop, so I relaxed. And then he drove it into my belly anyway. The red mist came down. I got back up and wore the hurl off him. Broke it across his arm. Then we ended up on the ground scuffling, helmets off.

'Let them at it! Let them at it!' I could hear Jackie shouting in the distance.

I had my fist clenched ready to bury him with a box and I don't know why I didn't but I just wrestled him instead. It ran its course, as these things always do, and we got up. But I was down on my haunches for ages afterwards as I was completely winded having not been braced for the belt. I was down for so long that Jack thought he had hit me somewhere else. 'I didn't mean to get you in the nuts,' he said. That's as close as there was to an apology from either party. My father was at training tonight and called me afterwards laughing his head off at the good of it.

I have no idea the last time something like that happened at club training, two lads going at each other. After the Mullinavat match, it was commented on at a team meeting that we weren't hard enough on each other at training. 'When's the last time a hurl was broke up here?' one of the lads wondered. I was in the shower afterwards and Séamus Dwyer came in with a smirk on his face. I just nodded at him and he walked off grinning. Given how we've been playing lately, a bit of aggro like that was no harm and I knew that's what Séamus was thinking.

####

With Kilkenny, it was obviously a more competitive environment and scuffles wouldn't happen terribly often, but there might be one or two a year, maybe. There was the one that I've spoken about already between Pádraig Walsh and me. Another night, Mark Kelly got Jackie with a flick and he just turned around and pulled across his head. It was wicked. Cody went ballistic. 'Jackie, do that again and you're gone!' Mark had a tendency to catch fellas with these flicks and one night he did it to JJ.

'I'm telling you now Mark,' JJ said matter-of-factly, 'if you do that again, I'm going to wear the hurl off you.'

And that'd be JJ. He'll give you one chance, he'll tell you about it and that would be it then.

Brian wouldn't be running in to break up these rows when they occurred. He obviously wouldn't want it happening every week but he wouldn't be unhappy at the odd one here and there. He'd let a fight run its course and then at the end of the session he'd say a few words to make sure it didn't affect the spirit within the group.

'Look, training is tough and we have to get each other ready for what's ahead. But we're all friends going off and we're all in it together.'

I remember once we were on a training camp in Carton House. Colin Fennelly wasn't on the panel all that long and he was being marked by Jackie, who was always going to try and take advantage of his greenhorn status. He gave Colin a wicked dirty belt and Cody let out a roar that was at once deadly serious and absolutely hilarious.

'Jackie, don't do it! Colin, get used to it!'

9

MAY

'I had played in 12 All-Ireland finals
with Kilkenny and I was never as nervous
as I was before this game'

Saturday, May 4, 2019

A week out from Kilkenny's first championship match against Dublin and Brian Cody has reported a number of injuries. Eoin Murphy, Conor Delaney, Cillian Buckley, Robert Lennon and James Maher are all out, while Richie Hogan will do well to get on the field. I can't ever remember it being this bad injury-wise during my time.

Brian generally had a tolerant attitude towards injuries but his patience would wear thin on occasions if the queue for the physio was growing a bit too long. 'If you're injured, you're injured, but if you have a niggle, just get the fuck out and train.' That'd fairly slash the queue for the next while. Just one of many examples of how he roots out mental softness. He wouldn't want lads who genuinely have issues to miss out on the treatment they needed, however, and sometimes after an outburst like that he'd pull me aside and say, 'Make sure you look after your groin and hip', just in case I'd be reluctant to have them seen to.

After my hip surgery in 2009, I had to manage it. A couple of years later I went through a period where I just had no power when I tried to sprint so I was sent down to Ger Hartmann in Limerick where both he and his right-hand man, Ger Keane, worked on me. Hartmann asked me to bring my right knee to my left shoulder but I could only barely steer it in that direction. 'You're all caught up,' he told me. 'It's like trying to close a door with three broken hinges.' He set to work on me and it was excruciating, but it worked a treat and after three sessions I was back to myself.

Over the years, Brian often cited Willie O'Connor as an embodiment of the sort of manliness that he expected of us. In the 2000 All-Ireland final, Willie suffered a broken rib and Brian was going to replace him but he insisted on staying on. 'I'll be grand, I mightn't hit a ball but neither will my man,' Willie said. 'That's the kind of attitude you need,' Brian would tell us.

Conor Delaney played at full-back for a lot of the league this year but his absence compounds the uncertainty that has surrounded that position since JJ Delaney retired after the 2014 All-Ireland win. Brian just hasn't been able to find a settled full-back over the past five years and, right now, nobody could say with any great certainty who'll be on the edge of the square in seven days' time. Between Noel Hickey and JJ, it was a position that knew nothing only stability for years. Noel was probably the better full-back, but JJ the better all-round defender.

Noel was quick and incredibly strong. It must be a farmer's thing from pulling calves and whatnot around the place. He read the game so well. Fearless. Some defenders would be wary of getting out in front in case they miss the ball but that just wasn't Noel. He bombed out to everything. I don't recall ever being marked by him at club level but at county training he'd give you loads of it.

In 2005 he had to sit out the latter stages of the championship after being diagnosed with a viral infection of the heart. He was a huge loss and his absence could well have cost us the All-Ireland. There's no way Niall Healy would have scored three goals off Noel Hickey in his prime in that year's semi-final. As it happened, the county board had tests carried out on all of us and poor Conor Phelan had to quit hurling completely after a leaky valve in his heart was discovered.

Thankfully Noel came back as good as ever, but then injuries started to mount for him and he missed out completely in 2009. By 2012 the edge had just been knocked off him a bit and forwards were able to run around him in a way they never could at his peak. Brian went with JJ as his first choice full-back at that stage. It was hard for Noel after the injuries and I think they dented his confidence, which in turn diminished Brian's confidence in him.

JJ was really the only player over the years that didn't endure tough love from Brian. Straight into the team in his first year out of minor in 2001, always selected when fit and then he went on his own terms after the 2014 All-Ireland final replay, with that majestic hook on Séamus Callanan a glorious sign-off. He's probably the only player who bowed out while knowing he almost certainly would have held his place on the team the following year. Of all the retirements over the years, that was the one that shocked me more than any other.

Brian described him as the best defender he'd ever seen after his cruciate injury ruled him out of the 2006 All-Ireland final and I'd be inclined to agree with him. Himself, Tommy and Henry were the three standout players from my time with Kilkenny. TJ Reid has moved into that company in recent years too and Eoin Murphy, if he maintains the levels of the last few seasons, could reach that level as well. JJ was the best defender and Tommy was the most skilful of the three but Henry was just the greatest when you tallied every quality that you'd want a hurler to have. If the Team of the Millennium was being revisited now, they'd all walk into it. We'd have other contenders too but nobody as nailed on as those three.

Although Tommy and JJ were both brilliant fielders, marking JJ presented a different challenge. When JJ was playing at full-back and marking me, he had this ability to bring his hurl up at the last second and, with a flick, clear everything out of his way and he'd be gone with the ball. Tommy was more subtle in that respect. Later in my career, when I was more experienced, I'd try and run around JJ as the ball was dropping in a bid to outfox him. He tended to just hold his ground but he'd be looking around to see where I was, whereas when I tried to run around Tommy it was a waste of time as he never stood still anyway; he was always on the move.

JJ played at full-back, corner-back and wing-back for Kilkenny though, strangely, he never got a run at centre-back, a position that I've no doubt he'd have been very comfortable in too. His best position was wing-back and, in fairness, it didn't appear to be the obvious call on Brian's part when he moved him to full-back, even though he shored it up back there. You need a good defender in there, he was strong in the air and mobile. Many's the time, like Callanan, I was left bewildered having thought I was well in the clear only to have my pocket picked. It wasn't all orthodox defending with JJ either, like when he blocked Eoin Kelly's goal-bound shot with his forearm in that 2013 qualifier game against Tipperary.

I remember the morning at training when he did his cruciate in 2006. It was horrendous. When someone got injured in a training match situation like that, Brian would usually just keep things moving along but everything stopped this time. JJ was on his own and in possession when he just let out this scream. I was coming up to my first All-Ireland final thinking, 'Oh my God, I can't believe this is happening.' I just felt that things were starting to crumble on us. We needed to throw everything at that Cork team and here was one of our best players in a heap. We played on for a few minutes but the session soon wound up; the bite was gone out of it.

However, it happened a couple of weeks out from the final so we had enough time to re-focus. Brian was always strong on that – next man up and just get on with it. It turned out to be a galvanising factor. I remember James McGarry saying in one of the team meetings coming up to the game that we'd wait for JJ and Donncha Cody, who was also injured, to join us for the team photograph on the day. JJ got back the following year and was picked up where he left off until he retired.

He went straight into punditry, like a lot of ex-Kilkenny players, and he'll be up in the studio in Nowlan Park next Saturday evening analysing the Kilkenny-Dublin game for *Sky Sports*. How Brian would love to have him out on the field again.

#####

There's a certain irony in my working for a media outlet now, albeit not quite in a journalistic role. The likes of JJ, Henry, Jackie and Eddie Brennan have all become television pundits and written newspaper columns since they retired. It's entirely natural that your attitude towards the media would change once you transition from player to ex-player, particularly in Kilkenny where our media dealings were kept to a minimum. Once freed from those shackles, former Kilkenny players have opened up to varying degrees.

While I was playing, I essentially took my mantra from Seán Cummins, who made the following declaration at a team meeting in 2006: 'Treat them like mushrooms – feed them shit and keep them in the dark!' Well, we all fell around the place laughing, but it stayed with me.

'You can say a hell of a lot but don't say anything at all,' Brian would tell us. It was like we were all subconsciously on message. My father would often say, 'Listening to Brian and listening to the rest of ye, there's no difference.'

I don't have to be so guarded these days but when you're

a player, you're in a bubble and everything revolves around winning. You don't want to utter a syllable that might give the slightest advantage to the opposition. While I was always careful about what I'd say, I was especially so after Jackie's interview with journalist Jackie Cahill was splashed across the papers after our league final defeat to Dublin in 2011.

It wasn't a good day for me personally having been sent off and Jackie labelled our 12-point loss as 'the worst performance I was ever involved in with Kilkenny', among other things. When he was called back by Brian at the end of the next training session, we knew what it was about. In fairness, everything he said was spot on but it didn't need a national audience.

There was further fallout from that game when the *Irish Independent* ran a headline 'Croker Chokers' in reference to us. Cody went absolutely ape over it. I've since been informed that the headline had nothing to do with the journalist who wrote the piece, Cliona Foley, but he was furious with her nonetheless. 'Who the fuck does she think she is?' Her name would have been mentioned in the dressing room more than once before that year was out and certainly not in glowing terms.

By and large Martin Fogarty managed our modest media dealings. 'Are you alright to do an interview? This lad will be ringing you.' Any phone calls from journalists outside of that were to be ignored.

Brian would have always told us that he doesn't read sports sections of the papers during the summer months, no matter what was on it. He felt it'd make you soft if you exposed yourself to that stuff. At various stages over the years he said, 'How many of them journalists would have hurled at inter-county or even club level?'

Social media became a factor then towards the end of my Kilkenny career. There wouldn't have been a huge emphasis placed on it within the camp, though we would have been warned about our postings all the same. But nothing would focus the mind in that respect more than an alert like: *Mick Dempsey is now following you.*

May has become a defining period of the year for inter-county hurling teams given the altered championship structure and the pivotal games that are now played at this time of year but throughout my career it was a month where we'd be winding ourselves up as our campaigns generally didn't start until June. Quite often we'd find ourselves in the league final on the May bank holiday weekend and then we'd head back to the clubs for a week or two before fine-tuning up to the first championship game.

It was like flicking a switch once you returned to the county panel ahead of the championship. The break after the league final was the line of demarcation. All the slogging that went with training before and during the league was done with. All that was ahead of you was summer hurling, dry fields and the pace of the game lifting noticeably. It was one of the most pleasant times of the year to be involved, though that dynamic is somewhat different now with Kilkenny in action about a month earlier than would have been the case throughout my time.

However, the build-up to the 2015 championship, my penultimate season with Kilkenny, was a pretty miserable one.

Indeed, my Kilkenny career came very close to ending a year and a half earlier than it actually did. I just couldn't get myself right. I was shattered all of the time. I was eating like a horse, sleeping soundly at night, but then I was also stretching out on the couch and nodding off for a couple of hours. And yet the tiredness wouldn't leave me.

'You may go to Tadhg,' Anne told me, 'that's not normal.'

So I contacted Tadhg Crowley, the Kilkenny team doctor, and he ran some blood tests. 'There's nothing showing up there,' he said. That was demoralising as I was feeling awful and there was nothing to explain it. A second blood test was done and there were still no answers.

I decided to pack it in as I thought that my body simply wasn't up to training at that level anymore. Tadhg had actually taken blood from me a third time but I wasn't prepared to wait for the results.

I literally had the phone in my hand standing out on the porch at home with Brian's name up, ready to call him and tell him that I was pulling out when Tadhg rang me. 'That other blood test that I took, it's showed up that you have glandular fever,' he said.

He put me on medication, I took a few weeks off and got back for our first game, the Leinster semi-final against Wexford. A few months after I'd been on the brink of quitting, we were All-Ireland champions again.

#####

Over the 12 seasons that I played with Kilkenny, we never lost our first championship game. Incidentally, we were beaten by Wexford first day out the year before I started in 2004 and again the year after I finished in 2017. The only year we didn't reach the Leinster final was 2013, when we had easily our worst championship campaign in my time. In retrospect, it's pretty easy to conclude why.

It was in the latter stages of that year's league that it emerged that Brian Cody was to undergo pre-planned heart surgery, which meant that he wouldn't be around for a few weeks and that Martin Fogarty and Mick Dempsey would be taking charge of the team. At that stage we were already in the groove and won the semi-final against Galway and then beat Tipperary in the final in front of a packed Nowlan Park, a game which we were never going to have any problems getting ourselves up for.

But as we regrouped for the championship, things weren't quite the same without Brian around and it's only really on reflection that I realised it. Just by being there, he's able to drag that extra five or 10 percent out of you. He doesn't have to say anything, his presence alone is enough. So his absence was huge. We were going for three-in-a-row again and there was nobody better than Brian at banishing that softness that can creep in when you've enjoyed success.

If he saw standards slipping in training, even slightly, he'd call us all in and fire out a few stern words. Everyone knew then. Mick Dempsey wouldn't exactly take prisoners in training either to be fair and he would have a bit of a fear factor about him, though Martin Fogarty was more the good cop. Neither of them could wield the same influence as Brian had over us though. By the time he came back, we were chasing our tails a little.

Throughout my time, we usually didn't tend to meet All-Ireland contenders early in the championship but that was irrelevant to our approach. We always wanted to be 100 percent from the first match to ensure that we weren't caught. If we started the championship in a letheragic manner we could find it difficult to pick it up as we went on, something that Tipperary, for example, were more adept at. They did it particularly well in 2010 and in 2014 to a lesser extent having lost their first outing. We felt it was far better to set off on the right footing and go from there but we could never find a smooth gait in 2013.

We played Offaly in our first game in Tullamore, a couple of weeks after Brian had returned. They were leading at half-time and though we won by five points in the end, we conceded four goals and were very sloppy. There was a debrief the following day in Hotel Kilkenny with every member of the panel called in individually. The weather was especially warm that summer and before I was called in I had gone for a swim and then into the sauna so the sweat was dripping off me as I sat down before them, though maybe that would have been the case anyway.

'What went wrong yesterday?'

'Do you think you're in good physical shape?'

'How do you think you're going?'

They weren't so much questions as statements. The rot had set in though. Dublin beat us after a replay. We lifted it against Tipperary and scraped through and then Waterford pushed us all the way in extra time before a Cork team that didn't do a whole pile before or after that sent us packing in the quarter-final. It certainly wasn't for lack of effort and we had injuries to key players that weakened us, but we were just that little bit off setting out on that summer and couldn't get back to ourselves. The core of the team was just past its best at that stage and that's why picking us up after 2013 to win the next two All-Irelands, with almost a patched-up side, is Brian's greatest feat.

#####

Saturday, May 11, 2019

You'd barely have known that Kilkenny were opening their championship campaign against Dublin this evening. My work takes me around the county but there was barely a peep about it all week. It's probably a reflection, to some degree, on the current championship structure whereby every team is guaranteed four games and the public is slower to engage when it's not do or die. Whatever it is about the Dublin hurlers, they aren't exactly box office either, though I was impressed by them against Limerick in the league semi-final. I thought before the game that they'd never get a better chance to beat Kilkenny and they certainly let an opportunity slip.

I was doing a championship preview segment in Brogan's Bar for *KCLR* today with Adrian Ronan, Aidan Fogarty and Oisín Langan and I was worried about the defence, particularly with Paddy Deegan named at full-back and Huw Lawlor centre-back, though I was a little unnerved by the whole half-back line to be honest.

Dublin should have been out of sight by half-time though they only led by four points. Kilkenny struggled big-time and Brian eventually moved Lawlor to full-back, Deegan to the wing and Pádraig Walsh to centre-back. Straight away, the defence had a much better balance to it. Pádraig dominated the second half and with TJ Reid orchestrating things up front, they outscored Dublin by 2-11 to 0-8 after half-time to win by five.

It was yet another example of Dublin falling asunder once the pressure was on. We always felt over the years that there was a soft centre with them. That if you could get on top of them when they're having a bad spell in a game, you could really bury them. They didn't have that Kilkenny-like mentality to be able to hang in when the tide was out and it was evident again tonight. Although they beat us in 2013, we generally tended to put them away without too much fuss.

There was a lot of hype about them in 2012 in particular, which we fattened on ahead of our meeting in Portlaoise. The feeling was that they were now ready to beat us but we crushed them, with Anthony Daly making his famous remark afterwards that 'if we gathered up 20 at the Red Cow and came down this morning it could hardly have been worse.'

The biggest talking point out of tonight's game was the bizarre incident shortly before half-time where Dublin maor foirne Greg Kennedy intercepted a free that TJ had attempted to play short to Billy Ryan. I've never seen anything like it in the game.

Kennedy was daft to poke the bear. The crowd reared up when it happened and there was a heightened level of hysteria about the place from there to the finish. It's difficult enough to win in Nowlan Park as a visiting team without riling the home support unnecessarily. Brian went bananas on the sideline at Kennedy and you can be sure it was referenced strongly in the dressing room at half-time. I was just imagining what he would be like.

'Who the fuck does that lad think he is, coming in and catching a ball when we had a goal-scoring opportunity. Go out and show them that they won't get away with that down here.'

Brian was always very good at gauging the temperature at half-time and saying the right thing. It wouldn't always be ram-it-down-their-throats kind of stuff either. I remember when we played Galway in 2014 in Tullamore, Andy Smith was doing his best to stir shit in the first half and some of our lads were standing up to him, not wanting to be seen to back down. 'Just forget about him,' Brian said when we got in. 'That's what he wants, he's trying to stop ye hurling, just forget about him and start hurling.'

Smith was a bit of a wind-up merchant and Brian's rationale was that if we took that away from him, he wasn't likely to hurt us thereafter.

#####

Wednesday, May 22, 2019

James Stephens 1-20 Ballyhale Shamrocks 1-9

A couple of weeks after the Mullinavat game, I was talking to Séamus Dwyer on the phone when he asked me where

I'd prefer to play. I thought of a conversation that I had with Philly Larkin last year. Philly told me that he had said to our management back then that they should consider playing me at centre-back because he felt we needed someone who would be able to win ball in the air and read the game. Nothing came of it at the time but when Séamus asked me, I told him it was something that I had been thinking about since the Mullinavat match.

'We have actually spoken about it,' Séamus said, 'playing you at centre-back has come up.'

I'd never played at centre-back in my entire career. Through the years, the club was always overloaded with backs and Jackie or Peter Barry or Philly would have filled the centre-back position for most of my time. We were never blessed with forwards in the club so I wasn't going to be shifted back when I was playing up front at inter-county level. But it's always been the most important position on the field in hurling and I was intrigued by the challenge at this stage of my career. I felt it could give me the shot in the arm that I needed, while helping the team too.

Séamus rang me a few days before we were due to play Mount Sion in a challenge game to inform me that I'd be wearing No 6 against them. Jackie had played there in our first two games but would be dropping to full-back. All in all, it worked well and we won comfortably though Mount Sion were very poor so I wasn't going to read too much into it. But I was excited for a game of hurling for the first time in ages.

It helped that I've played a lot at centre-forward so I knew what I didn't like a centre-back doing. I didn't overthink it though, I just slotted into the position and played my natural game by and large. There was one instance where I waited too long for a ball to drop and my man just came across me and flicked it down and was gone. You can't do that at centre-back. The next one that came down, I attacked it and held him off. Then I soloed upfield and belted it wide. The lads were slagging me afterwards. 'Jaysus, I thought you were going to do a Ciarán Carey on it!'

Carey was a centre-back that I really admired when I was growing up. I always liked Philly in that position too because he had great hands. He wasn't that big but was able to read the game so well. Brian Hogan was the best I played with though.

Last week we went to play Thurles Sarsfields in another challenge game, which I felt would be a much better gauge for James Stephens' new defensive alignment. They were better than Mount Sion but missing a few players all the same, I was told. I was happy with how I played again. I was probably a bit more composed than last time. Their centre-forward drifted off me a bit so Cian Kenny, who played minor for Kilkenny last year, came out and picked him up. Even when Cian wasn't there, I was speaking to the midfielders to pick him up. The main thing was to protect the centre of our defence.

I got in on the scoring too. I won a ball and played it to Tadhg Dwyer, who was standing in the centre-forward position. He collected it and moved off to the left and there was a space in front of me so I galloped forward seeking the return. He turned and handpassed it to me and I popped it over off my right. That was the only time I strayed from the centre-back area.

In all, the move had worked quite well and I knew that I

was going to be staying there for the next league game in Hugginstown this evening against Ballyhale Shamrocks, the All-Ireland club champions and a game for which I'd have TJ Reid as my direct opponent. Bit of a step up! I said to Séamus Dwyer after the game this evening that I had played in 12 All-Ireland finals with Kilkenny and I was never as nervous as I was before this game.

It was a hugely important game for our year. Not so much in terms of progression in the league, and with it the championship, but we struggle for consistency so much and having played well in the couple of challenge matches, to dip for this game would have been disastrous.

To be fair to Ballyhale, they were missing Colin and Michael Fennelly, Joey Holden, Conor Walsh and Brian Cody but I still think we would have beaten them anyway, just not as comfortably. We got on top early with the first five points before Adrian Mullen scored a goal for them. But we responded well and pulled clear again, hitting a few points before Eoin Guilfoyle added a goal. We were nine up at half-time and were comfortable in the second half, running out 11-point winners in the end. We didn't let them back into it, which we have tended to do in other games.

TJ had a frustrating evening but, while I had a decent game, I wouldn't begin to take the credit for that. He was drifting out to either wing and into the middle and with Cian coming out from corner-forward again, he picked him for most of the evening, allowing me to just read the game and pick up plenty of ball.

Cian's a feisty character for his age. He hurled TJ really well and even had the bravado to goad him while he was at it.

'You're overrated,' he told him. This from a young lad still in secondary school to arguably the finest hurler in the country! I've never really been one for the mouthing myself though I would have been a bit niggly, touching off my opponents and invading their personal space a little.

My pre-match nerves were partly informed by the fact that I feared a roasting off TJ, as any centre-back would. The game didn't pan out that way but then another part of me would relish the challenge of hurling on him for the hour. Maybe later in the year. In fairness to TJ, though, while he had a quiet game, it's very difficult at times to get yourself up for it when you come back to play a relatively meaningless club match, even though it was big for us, after performing heroics with the county team.

I was often in that position and I'd be really disappointed with myself. I was always my own worst critic but my father wouldn't be long weighing in with his appraisal all the same. 'It wasn't your best game today.'

We'd also have to acknowledge that the Shamrocks don't usually get too worked up for the league, even though it feeds into the championship. But we had a job to do tonight and we did it.

I had heard a bit of club talk in the run-up to the game about my new position. 'Why would you put your best forward in centre-back?' But I'm not our best forward anymore. Young lads like Eoin Guilfoyle and Niall Brassil have passed me out. They have more legs. I found that when I was in the forwards in previous games, I could win the ball but wasn't able to get anywhere with it. Moving to centre-back has re-energised me and when I think of it now, I wouldn't have minded going back there a few years earlier, though I'm not sure it would have been in the team's best interests at that stage.

I wasn't planning on going out after the game this evening but I was so satisfied with how it turned out that I went for a few pints. Séamus Dwyer wore the look of a relieved man. Joe Murray brought him to the game and said he never saw a man under so much pressure. Joe certainly didn't do anything to alleviate that when he said: 'You think you're under pressure now, imagine if we get beat by the Shamrocks and you're after playing the best forward the club ever had at centre-back!'

Thankfully that didn't come to pass. Murty Leahy even met Brian Cody on the way out of the match and asked him when he was bringing me back to play at No 6! Henry Shefflin came into our dressing room afterwards and was very complimentary about how I had played.

I'm certainly not getting carried away, though; there are far too many potential pitfalls for both the team and me, but tonight's game was definitely my most satisfying since I finished hurling with Kilkenny.

#####

Friday, May 24, 2019

Local election day. It could have been me! Driving around Kilkenny the past few weeks with faces on posters, it's a thought that naturally ran through my mind plenty of times but there were certainly no pangs of regret. Seeing my face and name on posters with 'Fianna Fáil' written under it would have been a bit weird, especially when I'm hardly a staunch card-carrying member of the party. I definitely made the right decision not to run.

Even a few weeks ago, a few of the local candidates came into the station for the *KCLR* Live show and Joe Malone, who approached me to run for Fianna Fáil back in October, got a bit of a hard time for his allegiances. 'You're running for Fianna Fáil, Joe?' scoffed presenter Eimear Ní Bhraonáin, who's not shy about grilling her guests when needs be.

'Yes,' answered Joe.

'The last time you were in you said you were going to run as an independent. Why would you say that?'

I was thinking, *I don't know if I'd have been able for that.* I certainly didn't feel I was missing out on anything today by not being involved. All the hassle of being out in the count centre over the weekend then; I don't think I'd have been ready for that sort of thing either.

While putting my face on an election poster was something I had reservations about, my mug will be more visible in the locality in the coming weeks in any event, just as the posters are coming down. I was approached a while back by a chap I know who has a company called Teamwear Direct which supplies all sorts of playing gear and training equipment for teams. He was wondering if I'd be interested in putting my name to a range of sliotars and we'd obviously divide the profits. So I said yes. My signature is printed on the balls along with the brand name, 'Eoin Larkin Hurling'.

They'll be going on sale in the local shops in the next few weeks and who knows what it might lead to. But I can hear the slagging already. 'If you're stuck for a few quid, Eoin, I'll look after you. You don't need to be selling balls in SuperValu...'

10

JUNE

*'There were days when I'd pull into the driveway
with no recollection of the journey I'd just been on.
The vacuum in my mind would be filled by negative
thoughts of the very worst kind'*

Wednesday, June 5, 2019

The strangest thing happened today: it rained. The weather gods always seem to be at their most antagonistic when the Leaving Cert exams get underway, but not this year. I know it was scorching when I sat mine seven years ago, just a month short of my 28th birthday and a full decade later than I ought to have been doing it. If only I hadn't left school after my Junior Cert.

The idea of belatedly sitting the Leaving Cert was first floated by my army colleague Mickey Comerford during the summer of 2011 when a notice went up in the barracks.

'Will we go down on that course?' he wondered.

'What? The Leaving Cert?'

'Yeah,' he said, enthusiastically. 'You'll be out of uniform for nine months, it'll be deadly, no duties or nothing.'

The course was offered through the Cork College of Commerce so we'd have to go down there to do it. I mulled over it. My cousin, Rory O'Donovan, who's also in the army, had done it the year before so I asked him about it and he gave it a positive review. Mickey and I deliberated over it a few more times up and down and eventually I said, 'Fuck it, we'll do it'. We applied and both of us were accepted.

Of course, my parents were amused at my going back to school. It presented my father with a handy free straight in front of the posts and he put it straight over the black spot.

'Oh that's funny, back to school?' he hooted. 'You wouldn't stay there when you were in it, you ran out of the place!'

They were supportive though, as was Anne, who thought it was a good opportunity. Brian Cody got a bit of a laugh out of it too when I told him.

To be honest, it started out as a bit of a doss for me but, at the same time, I knew that if I went down to Cork to do this, I was going to make a proper attempt at it. I took on five subjects: Irish, English, maths, geography and history. Mickey and I car-pooled, up and down to Cork every day, a drive of about an hour and three-quarters.

I had never carried an inferiority complex over the fact that I didn't finish school but then, with people knowing that I was going back to do my Leaving Cert, I became a little paranoid about it, fearing that I'd get poor results and that they'd then be quizzing me about how I got on, particularly the lads in the Kilkenny team. That fear drove me on a little. On the other hand, there was no great pressure on me.

I wasn't necessarily sitting the Leaving Cert to progress myself professionally, at least not at that time anyway. For the vast majority of those who started their exams today, it's a doorway to the rest of their career. They're depending on getting good results to get the course they want in college and it has knock-on effects for the rest of their life. But I had a job to go back to regardless of how my exams went.

I had come to regret my decision to leave school before I even started in the army. I was let go from a couple of jobs because the work wasn't there for me and couldn't get my apprenticeship finished. I had to sign on the dole. Immediately after leaving school I thought I was a great lad, earning a living for myself while the other eejits were still slaving away in the classroom. Then, there's a transition where they're going off to college and bettering themselves, heading for big jobs in cosy offices, driving a nice car while I'm out on building sites in the freezing cold, going around in a banger of a van with a heap of tools in the back of it.

'This is bullshit,' I'd growl to myself, 'why didn't I stay and do my Leaving Cert and get a degree?'

The other side of it is, while I was in school, I never really computed what college actually was, as hard as that might be to believe. It was just this vague extension of school that I didn't want to know about. I don't ever remember talking to a career guidance counsellor during my time in school. I failed to join the dots and see that college was a way of progressing yourself and getting a better job. I was just incredibly naive. And even when I joined the army, I hadn't a notion what I was getting involved in; that there was actually training involved. I thought you signed up and, just like that, you were a soldier. Imagine.

I would appeal to anyone who is considering packing in school to hang in there. I don't see how you'd possibly regret it. Go and talk to someone about it. In fairness, Mark and Holly are both in secondary school now and they're into it but they have their moments all the same.

'But sure, you left school at 15!'

'Yeah, exactly,' I reply, 'that's why I'm telling you to stick at it.'

What direction would my career have taken had I sat my Leaving Cert 10 years earlier? Well, if I had my time again I'd probably try and become a school teacher, albeit it would have been the irony to end all ironies had I signed up for a lifetime in school having resisted the idea of staying in it a single second longer than I had to when I was a teenager.

Teaching is certainly a career that lends itself to being an inter-county hurler though and we had plenty of teachers on the Kilkenny panel over the years; Richie Hogan, Cha Fitzpatrick, Michael Rice, Pádraig Walsh, Mattie Ruth. Work finishes reasonably early so you could get a nap in before training that evening if you wanted to, you had time to get all your food together for the week. In the summer you could get your gym and recovery sessions in with ease. But apart from the time off and how it would dovetail nicely with a hurling career, I think it's a job that I would have liked and excelled at, too.

In Cork, we weren't in a conventional school as such so we didn't have to share a class with teenagers; there were people of various ages. There were a number of people in the class who were drawing the dole and clearly didn't want to be there. There was a mass exodus after Christmas as they were no longer required to go to school to draw down the dole. But at least anyone who wanted to be there at that stage was there.

The teachers were all really pleasant, though I found the going tough initially, particularly with maths and Irish. From September to December I was constantly thinking, 'I'm not going to last nine months here.' It was different to what I felt when I'd been in school before; back then I was immature and I hated it, just because. This time I just found it tough. Intimidating. It wasn't easy going into an environment where all of this stuff was being thrown at you.

Once I got the Christmas break over me, however, I was fine. I had a new focus from January on. It was just like flicking a switch.

'Right, settle down here now, go into class and learn as much as you can.' And that carried me right through the rest of the year. Like, I used to get home in the evening at six o'clock and then do my homework.

When I was in school before, I'd often come in the door, throw the bag in the corner and not go near it again until the following morning, by which time I'd be panicking having not done any homework. To be honest, while I did my homework second time around, I didn't kill myself with study either, though as the exams drew close I stepped it up a bit; I was determined to do well.

I was captain of Kilkenny the same year and didn't miss a beat with the team through all of this and we were preparing for our championship opener against Dublin as I sat the exams. Once they came around, I was pretty relaxed; satisfied that I had put in more than enough work to cover myself.

When results day rolled around in August, I was doing a truck-driving course for the army in Clonmel. I pulled in at the side of the road and called up the phone number before punching in my code. I was shitting myself. It was a surreal feeling, me – me! – calling up and looking for my Leaving Cert results.

It was an automated system so the robotic voice droned out my grades: two A2s, a B2, B3 and a C1. 'Well, that's not right anyway,' I thought and swiftly hung up and made the call again, presuming I had put in the wrong code. But I hadn't. Same results second time around. I was absolutely delighted. Relieved, too. I rang Anne first and then my parents. They all congratulated me and told me how proud they were of what I had achieved, which was lovely. My father said he never thought he'd see the day.

Some time later, my English teacher, Susan Holland-O'Leary, emailed me to commend me for the effort I had put in all year and for my result, which she said was richly deserved. I wouldn't say that going back to do my Leaving Cert transformed my life, or anything like it, but it gave me more confidence, even though I hadn't felt diminished as a person for not doing it initially.

But it would have helped in terms of, say, writing my retirement statement when I was quitting Kilkenny or putting together a CV for the various jobs I've now had in the past couple of years. I wouldn't have been able to get into Pfizer, for example, if I didn't have my Leaving Cert.

For a while, when I was still in the army, I flirted with the idea of joining the guards, something that can be done while carrying over your service from the army. I never followed through with it but at least the option was open to me; it hadn't been before.

I didn't morph into a genius simply by sitting my Leaving Cert either and I certainly still have my limitations. When the kids ask me to help with their maths homework, I just tell them frankly, 'I haven't a clue about that' and that's fine.

It's funny actually, when the results came out that Wednesday in 2012 I was training with Kilkenny that night ahead of the All-Ireland final against Galway. After all I had been worrying about not doing well and having to face questions from the lads about my results, not one of them even asked me how I got on!

Thursday, June 6, 2019

I got my contract in *KCLR* today having completed three months' probation in the job. My manager, Marie Smyth, sat down with me to run through how I'd been doing. She was happy enough with my work and how I had integrated with the rest of the team. I have certain targets that I have to reach every month and I've been there or thereabouts with them, roughly in line with my colleagues.

I've been on air a few times on Friday and Monday mornings, looking ahead to and back on the weekend's hurling action, particularly from a Kilkenny point of view. They haven't managed to get an outside broadcast unit just yet, something which they planned on having around Kilkenny match days, so it looks as though it'll be next year before that side of the job really takes off for me but, all things considered, it's been a very good move for me and my family.

The army had its drawbacks and there were some difficult times while I was in it, but I was still happy in the Defence Forces for a long time. Professionally, this is the most content that I've been since.

After I returned from Syria in 2016, I had a bit of a lay-off before resuming work in the barracks. That's when my mood really started to plummet. I'd be driving in and out from our home in Callan, doing a school run or whatever, just daydreaming.

There were days when I'd pull into the driveway with no recollection of the journey I'd just been on. The vacuum in my mind would be filled by negative thoughts of the very worst kind. Suicide was one that became increasingly prominent, and appealing. Yet, it never occurred to me that, if I was thinking like this, there must be something seriously wrong with me.

Still, I'd generally come to my senses and consider my family at home, my parents and siblings. I'd think of funerals I've been at as a result of people taking their own lives. Like Niall Donohue's. The utter devastation. The emptiness in the eyes of the bereaved as I sympathised with them. Then I'd banish the suicidal thoughts from my mind. But they would always come back. And each time they did, they would swirl around my head that little bit longer. The more that happened, the more I began to rationalise ending it all.

Money would have been at the heart of that thought process. Anne and I were always struggling to make ends meet as we strived to do our very best for the kids. I reasoned that if I removed myself from the equation, the mortgage would be cleared through our insurance policy and Anne would have no problem providing for them without me. My self-worth was virtually nil. Eight All-Ireland medals? All Stars? Hurler of the Year? Part of the all-conquering Kilkenny team? Stop. These things wouldn't even enter my head.

I never circled a day in the calendar that I was going to do it. It was more like something that I was going to get around to. Like, say, when you plan on changing your car in the next couple of months.

All the while, I trained away with Kilkenny. But things within that set-up were grating on me as well. From when I first joined the panel up to around 2011, the standard of the training games was incredibly high. After that it slowly started to dip and that used to frustrate me greatly. Some lads just didn't realise what was expected of them.

In the later years, from around 2014 on, I felt the team became too much about Richie Hogan and TJ Reid. Now, I have great time for the two lads; they're absolutely superb hurlers, the pair of them. I remember when we played Wexford at Nowlan Park in the 2015 Leinster semi-final, Richie was bottled up in possession and I ran past him and shouted, 'Throw it out, Richie.' Well, he gave this inch-perfect handpass that landed right in front of me. I didn't have to break stride and clipped it over the bar. There was no fluke about it on his part.

But when he first came into the panel his shooting was a little wild at times and while he improved on that over the years, he still tended to take on shots rather than trying to work a higher percentage scoring opportunity. TJ shared that trait with him, I felt. When we were at our absolute peak some years before, the man in the best position always got the ball.

Before we played Dublin in the championship on June 11, we trained in O'Moore Park, where the game was fixed for. The lads got a bus up but I had been down in Tramore with the family so was allowed to drive. In a training game, I was in the full-forward line with TJ and we had a tactic where the inside three would pull back out the field and TJ ended up winning a few balls. I peeled off him a number of times waiting for passes that never came. He'd play a dummy pass and then lose the ball himself, whereas if he'd thrown it out, I had a handy point. Eventually, I lost it. 'Will you pass the fucking ball!' TJ told me where to go. I was getting increasingly thick as Brian wasn't pulling him up on it.

Later, an opposition puckout was played to my man and I didn't bother my arse pressing him as he cleared it down the field. Cody let a roar at me. Training finished up shortly afterwards, I went in, got showered quickly and jumped in the car. I had only driven a couple of hundred yards when the phone rang. You know who.

'Where are you?' asked Brian.

'I'm on the way home.'

'Come back, I want to talk to you.'

'I'm on the way home!'

'Come back,' he insisted, 'I want to talk to you.'

So I went back and met him and Mick Dempsey.

'What's wrong with you?' Brian wondered.

'Look,' I said, 'you never fucking say anything to him.'

'Who? TJ?'

'Yeah, TJ. You never say anything to him. If I didn't pass the ball and I lost the fucking thing, I'd know all about it. He's getting greedy, he just wants to score himself.'

Brian was aghast. 'What's your problem?'

'My problem is he won't pass the ball. He's putting himself before the team and you're putting him before the team.'

He tried to reason with me. 'Look, just relax now. You're only back from Syria and you're probably going to be playing next week, that's how much we think of you. There's not many lads that would come back and go straight into the team like that.' And it kind of petered out from there.

Again, TJ and Richie are great lads that have brought an awful lot to Kilkenny, but I just felt that we were drifting away from our core principle – that the team trumps all. In my opinion, the management had been sloppy in allowing that to happen. The lads weren't pulled up on things when I felt that I and others would have been in similar circumstances.

But the look of incredulity on Brian and Mick's faces when I pointed this out told me that they clearly didn't think this was the case. I'm not walking away from my conviction that this was a problem in our team, but was it irritating me more than it would have ordinarily given the mental state I was in? Yes, it was. I'd certainly never spoken to Brian like that before.

As he had intimated, I was picked to start against Dublin the following weekend, my first game for Kilkenny since the previous year's All-Ireland final. I would safely say it was my worst performance in a county jersey. If I'm honest, I was probably picked purely on reputation. Brian obviously thought he knew what I would bring to it but that was based on what I had done before, not what I was doing then. And, let's face it, he wasn't exactly weighed down with alternatives like he was a few years previously.

The game passed me by completely. I was barely on the ball. My touch was shite. Even when I was out in front, the ball was going everywhere. Dublin weren't up to much and we beat them comfortably but Eoghan O'Donnell cleaned me out. Roasted me while playing in a defence that was under pressure. At the time I would have tried to put it down to being a little bit off after coming back from Syria. Maybe that was a factor to a degree but, largely, it was wishful thinking on my part. I was taken off with 20 minutes to go. I thought it would have happened a lot sooner. I was embarrassed walking off the field.

The paranoia kicks in then. I didn't get any stick from supporters – that rarely happens in the GAA – but I was looking at people and drawing my own conclusions as to what they were thinking. 'That's it now, he's finished.' And in response to that I couldn't help thinking, 'Well, maybe I am.'

Still though, out I went that night. Once I'd get a couple in me, I'd be high as a kite and I'd glide through the night. The Dublin match was on a Saturday evening and I had taken the Monday off work, so I was straight out on the Sunday then as well. After I'd had my fill of pints, I'd hit the shorts and go flat out on the vodka, whiskey, Bacardi, whatever. I didn't drink to medicate and would never land into the pub on, say, a random Tuesday for no particular reason. But a few weeks before the Dublin match we were on our way to Anne's parents' house one Sunday afternoon when I just told her to drop me off at The Village Inn.

We'd been beaten by Dicksboro with the club the night before after we'd fallen asunder late on. So I stayed out all day and well into the early hours. That's not something I'd have done ordinarily. Banging hangover the next day. It was the same after two days of it following the Dublin game. Going on shorts was a trigger for my depression, which I didn't notice at the time.

Come the next morning, I didn't want to see the world beyond my bedroom.

The blankets would be pulled up over my head and I'd stay there for the day as the gloom descended further.

######

Friday, June 14, 2019

The life of a club player. Our win over Ballyhale Shamrocks gave us a tremendous boost but there's no opportunity for us to surf the momentum. That's because we don't have another game of consequence until the weekend of August 31. That'll be more than three months without a meaningful match. In some ways, at this stage of my life and career, it suits me as it gives me more time to recover and I can plan various things that I want to do over the summer but, in general, it's a highly unsatisfactory situation and it's replicated across the country because of the predominance of the inter-county game.

Laois dual player Cahir Healy was the subject of an excellent interview with Michael Verney in the *Irish Independent* today where he called for the GAA to stop putting the cart before the horse with the club and county. He believes that players should train with their clubs primarily and then be released to play with their county ahead of games, similar to the model that's there for international soccer and rugby. He's dead right.

It's become far too skewed towards the county and I'm not exactly blameless myself. There were times, occasionally, where I would miss a game with the club because I had a slight injury and wanted to make sure that I was right for an upcoming Kilkenny match. That's not right either and is not something I'm proud of.

Now that I'm a club player only, it's difficult to keep myself ticking over for the summer and I don't like the idea of easing off and then building myself up for the end of August as then there's a danger of me going mentally soft. That's partly why I pulled my hamstring the other night. I was doing 24 runs of 80 metres and by the time I did the 23rd I could hear my almost 35-year-old body telling me that I'd done enough. I didn't listen and did my hamstring on the 24th run.

A few of our lads have decided to head off for the summer and I can hardly blame them. A couple have gone to America. While I did two tours of duty, it's not something I ever really had the opportunity to do. Realistically it was never going to happen after having the kids when I was still quite young myself but, in any event, I'm not sure that spending a summer in America would have been for me.

In 2013, Mick Fennelly and I went out for a long weekend

to play in the New York county final for Galway against Tipperary. We went up to Dublin the night before we were to fly out and stayed with Richie Hogan. Of course, the two of us ended up in Copper Face Jacks and, sure enough, missed our flight the next morning and had to catch a later one. It was the only year we didn't at least reach an All-Ireland semi-final during my career so there was never an opportunity to go and do something like that before or after.

I have to say it was weird putting on the Galway colours. When you think of the set-up out there, it's a bit ridiculous: two lads like us with absolutely no affiliation to Galway whatsoever going out to play for them in New York purely on a one-off basis in their biggest game of the year.

Tipperary had been knocked out even earlier that year so they had quite a few lads playing against us in the final, which they won. The standard was pretty good but I knew no one on the team other than Mick. We had a great few days and were treated well. We barely put our hands in our pockets and were thrown a few quid for playing the match. I certainly wouldn't begrudge lads of it, but it's a wildly different experience to playing hurling or football in Ireland.

There's a bigger picture that the GAA needs to see with the fixtures programme though. They can't keep taking lads for granted.

For people like me, there was never a likelihood that my head would be turned by other sporting pursuits but if you're a young player now and you're handy at a few different sports, it's easy to see how you could drift towards the code that offers you a far more stable programme of fixtures. The summer is stretching out before us now but the serious club hurling won't get going again in Kilkenny until the evenings are fading badly. That's not sustainable.

######

Sunday, June 16, 2019

Galway and Clare, two of last year's semi-finalists, gone out of the championship this weekend. Waterford have long since been wiped out. Limerick into the Munster final against Tipperary despite losing to them today. Kilkenny and Wexford to contest the Leinster final after drawing last night.

I am surprised that Tipperary have done as well as they have and they've been seriously impressive but I still have my doubts about them. The writing was on the wall for Clare after they were wiped out by Tipperary and Limerick and it's been another disastrous showing for Waterford this summer.

They still have the core of a young team to be able to bounce back from this but one thing they need to do is find a settled position for Austin Gleeson. The games have largely passed him by. When we played Mount Sion a few weeks back one of their lads said that they were planning on picking him at midfield and just leaving him there. Waterford could do worse.

It was widely assumed that Galway were back on track after beating Kilkenny in Nowlan Park last week but even then I wasn't convinced by them. They were still only hurling in patches. It says a lot that they were hanging on to win that game by a point. Yes, they've been without Joe Canning up until his cameo off the bench in the defeat to Dublin last night but they've had 15 players on the field at all times. I would question just how good this Galway team has been because when they won their All-Ireland it was against a Waterford team that hadn't done a huge amount before that and have done nothing since. I still thought they'd beat Dublin but was I shocked that they lost? No.

It definitely would have hurt Brian Cody to lose a championship match in Nowlan Park. It was the first time it had happened in 70 years, albeit Kilkenny hadn't played too many home games in the interim. They hung in and fought to the end but the team clearly has its limitations at the moment. They played better against Wexford last night and probably should have won the game. As one wag said to me after the Galway game, 'We'd be Carlow without TJ.' I wouldn't quite go that far, but I can see where he's coming from at the same time.

######

TJ wasn't at his best in Wexford Park but he's been at such a high level for Kilkenny for the past few years now that the average performances seem conspicuous.

There has been talk lately that he's now one of the best forwards to have played the game and he's certainly in that company. He has everything: strength, ball-winning ability and he's deadly accurate. Moreover, there's huge pressure on him now, more than there ever was on Henry Shefflin, because if he doesn't play well and put up a big score, Kilkenny are going to find it very hard to win. A bit like Kilkenny in that mid-'90s period with DJ Carey.

You could pose a question as to whether TJ would be as influential as he is right now if Henry was still around and at his peak; that Henry's presence might not allow him to wield the same influence. I don't buy it. I'd say that he certainly would be as good as he is and possibly even better with Henry around because he wouldn't be carrying the weight of the team to anything like the same degree.

It's a point that was often made about Richie Power in relation to being in Henry's shadow though, again, I wouldn't indulge it. Richie had talent to burn, more than any of us, but he didn't have the application that Henry had. He loved hurling but just wasn't a fan of training.

Brian and Mick Dempsey would have been on to him quite a lot over the years just to push himself that bit more. That's not to make light of the injury problems that he had over the years because he was extremely unfortunate in that respect and could well be still playing at the highest level today only for them. He had to endure tough love from Brian at times in the early years, as many did, but he got a good run at it around 2010 and '11 when he was in the team and largely injury-free and won his two All Stars.

But he had been reduced to cameo roles by the time he was forced to quit due to his knee problems after the 2015 All-Ireland. He came back towards the end of the 2014 championship and started the draw and replay against Tipperary. By 2015, his only appearance was as a second half sub in the final against Galway. I think he was only able to train with us once – once! – all year and yet he got on a ball straight away and sprayed a perfect cross-field pass to Mick Fennelly.

When he retired a few months later, many of the tributes directed at Richie from his teammates referenced him as the most skilful player of all they had played with. It's hard to argue with that. He had an incredible touch. I always knew that if I played a ball to him, he would control it. You could make another run safe in the knowledge that you wouldn't have to check your stride to allow for any sloppiness on his part. The fact he could sit out a whole year and slot in seamlessly at the business end of the season – and that someone like Brian would have the faith in him to do it – says it all really.

There were instances in training where you'd be gasping at some of the things he could do. I remember he was on JJ one evening and he held him off as the ball was about to go over his head, flicked it down into his hand, pushed JJ away and laid the ball off. A breathtaking flourish that married his physical strength, skill and vision.

######

I could still see Kilkenny, on their day, beating everyone that's left in the championship with the exception of Limerick.

Physically, I just don't believe that they'd be able to compete with them. Tipperary are stronger than Kilkenny personnel-wise but I could see Kilkenny getting under their skin again. Mentally, they'd definitely have the edge on them. Then you have Cork, who are hit and miss.

The Leinster final is important for Kilkenny. It's a direct route to the semi-final and there are a raft of players there that don't have Leinster medals and it'd be a real boost to their confidence to win one.

I won my first in 2005 and it was a big day for me because I scored three points in a nervy win over Wexford having had a bit of a nightmare in the semi-final against Offaly, my championship debut. We scored 6-28 and won pulling up but I made no impression at all. So while it might have looked like just another Leinster title for Kilkenny, it was my first and a very important milestone in my career having contributed in a tight game. God knows when I'd have been given another chance if I hadn't.

The 2011 Leinster final was also a significant one personally because I had been sent off for the only time in my Kilkenny career in the league final against Dublin, who we faced again in the provincial decider. Conor McCormack had been marking me in the league final and when he pinched me on the neck I reacted by instinctively drawing back and hitting him. It looked like I had just pulled on him when I hadn't really. Anyway, Michael Wadding sent me off and we were beaten by 12 points in the end. It was a woeful performance though we hadn't been playing well that spring, had stumbled into the final and were missing a host of key players, who were back by the time the Leinster final came around.

We didn't tend to lose consecutive games to the same opposition in my time with Kilkenny. Cody would feed us snippets on the previous beating in the run up to the next meeting and that Dublin game in 2011 was a perfect case in point. Bits and pieces here and there and then we could be out on the field one night pucking around ahead of training and we'd all be called inside and told in no uncertain terms that another such showing wouldn't be good enough. We beat Dublin by 11 points in that Leinster final and I did well, scoring 1-2. The 2014 Leinster title win was satisfying too because we hadn't won it in three years at that stage, just like the current team.

I have 10 Leinster medals and while we often weren't pushed to the brink to win those titles, they certainly mean something to me. When I was growing up Leinster finals were huge events and I dreamt of winning one. The upcoming final is a bit of a throwback to that era because it's a genuine 50-50 game again and Kilkenny's season probably hinges on it.

######

Sadly, Amanda Stapleton died last month. I couldn't make the funeral but I sent her brother Paddy a Mass card. She was just 31, a shockingly young age. It brings to mind the passing of my aunt, Anna Norris, my mother's sister, in March of last year following a similar illness.

Anna lived roughly twice the life that Amanda did, however, and had the opportunity to leave a rich legacy in the shape of her three children, my cousins, and she was fortunate enough to stave off cancer when it first took hold of her 14 years earlier. There's some comfort in that, even if she passed all too soon in the end. For Amanda, it was far more abrupt and my heart goes out to her family.

11

JULY

'How are you feeling this morning?'

Monday, July 1, 2019

I think I completed the transition from Kilkenny player to supporter yesterday. The Leinster final was the first time that I had watched the Kilkenny senior team in Croke Park since I was with the minor team for the 2002 All-Ireland final. I was excited and nervous, which hasn't been the case for any of the games I've been at since I retired. I've tended to be more passive.

It makes sense, I suppose, when you think about it. You're never going to go from being a long-serving player to a hyperactive supporter straight away. Not that I was jumping out of my skin yesterday, but I suppose you could say that I was on the edge of my seat.

TJ Reid scored a delightful point in the second half when he turned Wexford's Kevin Foley inside out with a dummy. I had the fist clenched. I wouldn't have been like that at Kilkenny games before then. When Mark Fanning scored what turned out to be the winning penalty for Wexford, it was like a knife through the heart. It must have been the Croke Park factor. I barely knew how to get to the ground to be honest.

Anne was supposed to come with me but then couldn't as she had to bring Ellie to a dancing event. So I ended up driving up on my own.

My uncle, Jim Donovan, and some cousins were in the Hill 16 pub so I parked the car and met them in there to watch the Munster final. Limerick completely steamrolled Tipperary in the end and I think it could knock the stuffing out of them. They didn't have reinforcements on the bench and Limerick made light work of them in the end.

You'd have to be hugely impressed by Limerick. I know they've lost a couple of games this summer but they've learned their lessons and I don't see them being stopped. When you look at their side, the average age is younger than that of ours when we won in 2006. They could do four-in-a-row themselves if that team stays together. They have youth, power and pace in abundance, while they can score from all over the field.

When we were leaving the pub I had to hang back for my uncle Jim because I didn't know whether to turn left or right when we were going out the door. Any time that I went to Croke Park with the Kilkenny team, we'd be coming in from the Crowne Plaza Hotel after our pre-match meal and I'd be chatting or snoozing, oblivious to how we got there. We walked up together but his tickets were for the Hogan Stand

and I was in the Cusack. 'You're going that way so, are you?' said Jim. 'Eh, yeah,' I said, unconvincingly. I wandered on but once I could see the ground I was able to figure out where I was going.

The result didn't go Kilkenny's way and while I was very disappointed with the outcome, I still had a really enjoyable day. What used to turn me off going to games in Croke Park was the hassle of getting up and back but it was something I had overestimated. I just drove up, parked the car without too much fuss, went to the pub, went to the game and then drove home, with no great traffic despite more than 50,000 being in attendance.

Since I retired, I could take or leave Kilkenny matches but now I've caught the bug again. I'll be on holidays for the quarter-final, but I'll definitely go to the semi-final if they make it.

#######

It's interesting how Brian Cody has belatedly developed the habit of selecting dummy teams, something he never did in my time. He's clearly trying to get an edge and it's a veiled acknowledgement that the team, while not struggling, is not nearly as formidable as it was. He's trying to exploit any advantage that he can

At our peak, it never happened. You might get positional switches but by and large the team that was released on a Friday night was that which took the field on the Sunday. Brian knew he was playing a strong hand. He was throwing the gauntlet down to the opposition. It's different now.

241

It didn't look like a Brian Cody team yesterday. I would say there are a number of players starting that aren't Brian Cody players. Six, maybe more. I'm wide open to accusations of club bias here but Conor Browne strikes me as a Brian Cody player and he's not getting a look in. He wouldn't be the most naturally gifted but he can hurl, he can move and he's built like a tank. A real man, in the Cody mould. He could play wing-back or midfield, where he starred for us against Ballyhale a few weeks back. I'm convinced he could make the step up.

Brian's options are limited to some degree, particularly with the injury problems he's had, so he can't just discard half of the team but I'd expect him to freshen it up a bit for the next game. Anyone can lose on a given day but they really ought to have been beating Wexford. They didn't inflict enough damage on them when the momentum was in their favour and they didn't limit it sufficiently when it was flowing against them.

#######

The way that Wexford play presents a different tactical challenge and, though they only won the match narrowly through a late goal, I would say that they dictated the game to Kilkenny for the most part.

Brian always swatted away questions about tactics from the media but while the refrain that 'Kilkenny don't do tactics' wasn't entirely true, they weren't as prevalent as many might have believed. From when I started to when I finished, the tactical side had developed significantly but not in an overbearing way. I would think that Mick Dempsey had a strong input in that respect but, while I obviously can't say for certain, I'd imagine tactics were a more prominent topic in other dressing rooms than in ours.

For a long time, tactics were a luxury that Brian may have felt we didn't need to indulge in to a great degree. He knew that if we hurled to our ability we were going to win no matter what the opposition did. But that hasn't been the case with Kilkenny for a few years now.

Puckouts is an area where the game has shifted dramatically. When I was starting out, the message was to 'win your own ball', which always went long. Over the years though, that mantra changed to 'we have to be smarter with possession'.

Short puckouts were made fashionable by Donal Óg Cusack and Cork but it was years later before we started to use them and, even at that, it was more an occasional thing. It didn't start because Brian swept into training one evening and announced that we were going to go this way. In fact, it was a very gradual thing.

The goalkeepers might have tried a few at training on a particular night and then when one would break down the cry would ring out, 'No more short puckouts, puck it out!' And that would be that for a while until it would make inroads at training again and then, eventually, you'd get the odd one in a match and on it went from there. But it was never a case of being told to go short for a puckout. Brian would trust the goalkeeper to do what he thought was right and when you have someone of Eoin Murphy's ability, it would be foolish to stifle the range of striking that he has.

That Cork team from 2003-06, with their short puckouts

and running game, was an example of how Brian reacted to a trend in the game. It would generally take a loss or a bad performance for us to really zone in on something tactically and adapt.

It's evolved a fair bit even since I stepped away. I remember going to a league game, not long after I had finished, and I couldn't believe what I was seeing. Cillian Buckley collected a short puckout and handpassed it to Paddy Deegan bursting past him and Paddy played a short stick-pass from there. Win your own ball?

With the advent of sweepers, some nights in training an extra defender would be thrown in but that's as far as I can ever see Brian going down that route. I just couldn't imagine him using a seventh defender in a game situation. I don't think that's down to pride or stubbornness, he just looks at the game a different way to some other managers. Ultimately I don't think you're going to win an All-Ireland playing like that. Even when Clare won in 2013, they played man-on-man against Cork in those finals.

While I played most of my hurling for Kilkenny at left half-forward, in the latter part of my career I was named at corner-forward but given a licence to roam, though I wouldn't describe the role as that of a sweeper. Brian just told me to go where I wanted, to hunt the ball. I could end up in our own full-back line but the thinking behind it was to have an extra body around the middle of the field, which was becoming increasingly clustered in the modern game. He felt that I'd be able to get on the ball and give a good pass inside when I did. When I played at wing-forward I would have drifted too but not to the same extent.

Generally, if things had stayed the same, I think Brian would have stayed the same but that's not to say that he wouldn't embrace change enthusiastically once he thought it was for the benefit of the team. Things like video analysis, statistics and GPS units might have been commonplace elsewhere before we turned to them, but they certainly weren't introduced for the sake of it.

For all that though, the thrust of Cody's team talks was what changed the least over the years. Whatever tactical snippets he had to impart, it'd invariably wind up with something like, 'What I say here is irrelevant, a match can take on a life of its own so ye need to just do the right thing at the right time.'

#######

Of the five games Kilkenny played in the 2016 championship, Brian made just 12 substitutions, less than half of what was available to him, which spoke louder than anything about the dearth of options available to him relative to a few years before as the four-in-a-row team petered out.

Even when we were winning comfortably coming down the stretch against Dublin and Galway, the bench wasn't emptied, while Michael Fennelly's ruptured Achilles against Waterford was obviously an enforced substitution and certainly wouldn't have been made otherwise with the game on a knife edge.

I was involved in four of those 12 substitutions, either coming or going. Somehow I managed to keep my place for the Leinster final against Galway despite my limp effort against Dublin. If it was a few years earlier and I had played like that, I'd have been looking in at the match the next day, without a doubt. But my performance was just as bad against Galway, probably even worse. I was gone at half-time which at least spared me the walk of shame. Of course, the paranoia kicked in again as thoughts that I was washed up resurfaced, sinking my mood further. They stuck with me throughout the evening until after the post-match meal, when I had a couple of pints to take the edge off me.

The dynamic within the Kilkenny panel had changed for me at that stage. On any team, faces come and go and most of the ones that I was closely associated with were gone by then: Brian Hogan, David Herity, JJ, Taggy, Tommy, Henry. Jackie was still there but he had his own stuff going on that year between shaking off injury and trying to get back in the team. Now, I had no personal issues with anyone in the panel but, outside of Jackie, none of them would have been close friends of mine, per se. There was just a bit of a generation gap, I suppose, with virtually all of those who were there when I first came in now gone.

So the same support network wasn't there for me in 2016. I'm not saying that I would have sought counsel from all or any of those lads if they were still there, that wouldn't be my style, but they would have been looking out for me, I suppose. They would have come and tried to cheer me up after the rough run of form.

I didn't have that in my last year with Kilkenny. That's not to point the finger at anyone who was involved, it's just how panels naturally evolve and an upshot of that was that I was left somewhat isolated. But, of course, that didn't stop me getting right in the thick of it for the drinking session on Sunday night and Monday which left me in a depressive heap once again on the Tuesday morning after another shorts-fuelled binge.

I didn't go to work at all that week. We had a club match on the Friday evening against Fenians of Johnstown in Castlecomer. I didn't go to training on the Tuesday night and didn't even have the manners to tell Niall Tyrrell, our manager. I just sent a text to Joe Murray, a selector, saying that I wasn't going. It was very bad form on my part. The club have to go without their county players for so much of the year and then when we're expected back ahead of a championship match, I just didn't bother my arse turning up. In fairness, I don't think anyone could have ever reasonably accused me of going through the motions with the club when I came back off county duty, I always did my best for James Stephens, but I was only a shell of a man at that time.

I turned up for the game that Friday night. I slumped into the dressing room, didn't say boo to anyone, got togged out, sat down and waited, staring into space with my legs crossed until it was time to go out on the field. Usually I'd be one of the talkers in the club dressing room, but I didn't utter a word. I started full-forward. I had zero interest. If the ball came to me, I went and got it, but I wasn't doing anything beyond the bare minimum, if I was even doing that much. I just couldn't wait to get out of there.

Despite all that, I still scored 1-1. The goal was quite a good one, actually. A high ball came in and I caught it as I moved across the goal. It was a tight angle but I whipped it in the net. Then I walked back to my position. There was absolutely no elation on my part whatsoever. If the shot had gone wide or been saved or hit the post, I would have felt exactly the same.

There was one stage in the game when I belatedly decided to chase a Johnstown player in possession. I should have been closer to him to ensure he didn't get the ball in the first place but I was standing well off him. As I gave chase, trying to get a hook in, James Tyrrell came in and I warned him, 'Don't foul him, don't foul him' before he gave away a free. 'Fuck sake James!' I growled. It was right in front of our management team.

'No it's not James, that's you!' roared Niall Tyrrell.

'Ah just fuck off, will ya,' I shot back before walking back up the field.

Again, that's just not my form. Brian Cody was a selector that year and was standing right beside Niall, who was right, of course, but I just didn't want to hear it. We won well in the end and I got out of there as quickly as I could. I drove home and went to bed. Even the lure of a session with the lads didn't appeal. There was no hangover from hell the next morning but it didn't make any odds: I still felt like shit.

At around 11am, the phone rang. Brian Cody. I looked at it for a couple of seconds, pondering whether I should answer or not. Eventually, I did. And it only took the simplest of questions for the emotions that had been dormant for so long to gush from me like a geyser.

'How are you feeling this morning?'

I immediately burst into tears. I wasn't just misty-eyed or a little bit emotional, I was full on bawling my eyes out with Brian Cody on the other end of the phone, to the extent that I was unable to communicate with him for the most part. Brian tried to fill the vacuum.

'Look, there's obviously something bothering you. I could

see it in your body language last night. You weren't focused on anything… Even though you're feeling like this, you were still able to do that last night,' he said, referring to the goal I scored.

'Is it to do with last week?' he wondered, referencing the Galway game.

I finally managed to blurt something out.

'I don't know, Brian. I really don't know.'

'Look, Tadhg is there, give him a ring. I don't have to know anything about it, it can be between you and him. If you want help from me, there's no problem. If you don't want me to know about it, it can just be between yourself and Tadhg.'

The phone call lasted three or four minutes, maybe. You couldn't really call it a conversation because that requires at least two participants and I was largely unable to engage with him in a coherent manner. Brian was conscious of that so the phone call eventually wound up with me agreeing to give Tadhg a ring.

Brian took it all in his stride. He would have decided to ring me knowing that there was something wrong based on what he had seen the night before and was quite calm throughout the phone call. There is a perception that he's some sort of callous and obdurate individual and while it's true that he has a low patience threshold for bullshit, there is a lot of compassion to the man too. I experienced it that Saturday morning. I was grateful for it. Because that phone call was the moment on which everything turned for me.

Anne had been going in and out of the room until she noticed how upset I was while on the phone. I'm a closed book, I don't show that sort of emotion. Not even to her.

So, naturally, she was taken aback. She had been the one person that was telling me for years that I was depressed and I wouldn't listen. But it was only there and then that she would have realised the full extent of it. I was still in ribbons after getting off the phone and was physically unable to ring Tadhg. So she called him for me and we went down to see him together.

Tadhg's a hugely popular figure within the Kilkenny set up. He'd be more one of the lads than one of the management. So it wasn't like I was going in to a stranger, but it was still difficult. Anne did the talking initially when we got there, taking Tadhg back through the previous few weeks, months and years even. Then he turned to me and asked me a few questions. I was still shaking with the tears as I told him I had been considering suicide.

'Have you anything planned?' he asked.

'No, but it's constantly going through my head, when I'm driving the car or if I have a few minutes when I'm daydreaming – that's what comes into my head.'

Tadhg prescribed me a couple of diazepam to take the edge off me as well as antidepressants.

'I'm not saying you can't drink anymore but just cut it out for a couple of weeks,' he said. 'You'd be better off staying away from training and staying out of work. Just concentrate on getting yourself feeling better. If you want to go out and do a bit of exercise, by all means go out and do it and keep yourself busy around the house. Don't be lying in bed all day.'

We went home and my parents called around together later that evening; Anne had been in touch with them. With the diazepam, my eyes were a bit weird.

'You look out of it, what's going on?' my father asked.

'Look, I'm just feeling shit, end of story.'

Even then, I wouldn't just come out with it.

My mother was more diplomatic, but I could see the concern, and a bit of shock, in both of them. They just wanted me to be ok.

'Won't you ring me now if you want anything?' my mother said to me. I think she was almost afraid to leave me in case I did something.

I was zonked out of it due to the medication but I had definitely turned a corner. Unlike when I went to the doctor with Anne a few years previously just to get her off my back, there was buy-in from me this time. Brian's phone call was the catalyst. It helped lift a weight off my shoulders. It allowed me to realise that yes, there is something seriously wrong with me here. And you can only fix a problem once you accept that you have one.

I regret that I didn't have that moment of clarity sooner, that I couldn't just see what was wrong with me when the signs were so blindingly obvious. And, I suppose, if you're bawling down the phone to Brian Cody and you don't realise that there's something up, then I guess you never will.

The other side of it is, I'm thankful that it happened at all because if it hadn't and I had carried on as I had been for another few weeks or months, there's every chance that I would have taken my own life. I'm fortunate that there was that intervention from somewhere.

Prior to that, I didn't communicate with anyone as to how I was feeling and what was going on inside my head. Express my feelings? No way. It's frightening to think that I was going through such despair, yet I had no idea that I was depressed and refused to even entertain the notion that I was until that day, July 9, 2016.

But July 10 was a little bit better. And July 11 was a little bit better again.

#######

Tuesday, July 9, 2019

'Jesus, is it three years? Doesn't feel like that at all,' said Anne when I reminded her today, the first day of our two-week family holiday in Costa Calma, Fuerteventura. We've never taken a holiday quite this long before. We booked it last August and paid it off bit by bit. With a 5.40am flight, it required us to be on the road by 1.30am. We'd all been looking forward to it though Ellie was really bouncing with excitement, like it was Christmas Eve. 'I can't wait until tonight, I can't wait until tonight!' she kept saying yesterday.

She set her alarm even earlier than ours this morning but, of course, when I went in to her she was fast asleep having knocked it off. 'It was going off for about half an hour,' said Holly in the bed beside her. Mark was awake before any of us and ready to go.

We stopped for a coffee on the way up and met the two other families that we're travelling with at the airport. The Rodgers sisters, Siobhán and Sinéad, and their respective husbands, Mark Walsh and John Shiel, are friends of ours and they've come with their children as well, so it should be a great couple of weeks, all told. It's all-inclusive and the hotel is fantastic, opening out onto the beach. It's been a long day but once the kids hit the pool they were re-energised.

Up to when we got to the hotel, I frequently thought about where I was three years ago compared to now and the obvious contrast. Then I just parked it and looked ahead. We're really going to enjoy these next two weeks.

#######

Wednesday, July 17, 2019

Thirty-five today. Anne didn't even remember it at first this morning. Holly came into our room and wished me a happy birthday and then she shrieked, 'Oh Jesus!' I'd have been shot if it was the other way round! There isn't much fuss around my birthday anyway and I'll get whatever presents are coming my way once we get home.

The reason that it slipped her mind was because she was so wound up trying to get everyone organised for breakfast so that we could catch a bus at 9am to the Oasis Wildlife Park. To be honest, it's not the way I'd wish to spend my birthday or any other day for that matter.

We often go to zoos and the like as a family but it's just not for me. If we're watching television back home and there's something on that involves any sort of cruelty towards or oppression of animals, Anne always winces, something I reminded her ahead of this excursion.

'Sure this is the very same thing,' I told her.

'This is different, they're after saving them,' she insisted. 'They'll never be reintegrated into the wild.'

'Well they won't reintegrate them anyway if you keep giving them money!'

Ellie came to me yesterday and said, 'You get to hold a snake for your birthday!' No thanks. I can't stand snakes or any reptiles, come to think of it. I tagged along anyway and went through the motions but when they decided they were going to hang out with lemurs for a full hour I bailed out and got a taxi back to the hotel with Mark Walsh as his young lad, Liam, needed a nap.

Other than that, the holiday has been really enjoyable so far. There's a lovely routine to the whole thing. We get breakfast and hang by the pool until about five in the evening, have dinner at six and then a few drinks in the evening. It's terrific value and everything we need is on site; we needn't necessarily leave the place at all. All the kids are getting on great together too.

The thoughts of going home aren't terribly appealing. We're all agreed on that, even Anne, who's a real homebird. When we went to Florida a few years back it was grand, but we were happy to get home when the time came. It was similar with the Kilkenny team holidays. They were unbelievable craic but I'd only be a shell of a man by the end of them and the respite was welcome. This is different, much more leisurely, and would get you thinking about the future. For a couple of our age, the children are relatively grown up and it'd be great to go and live in the sun for a few months of the year once we're retired.

But never mind a few months, two weeks like this is more than we've ever had as a family before. Summer holidays just weren't an option when I was playing for Kilkenny. Was it worth it? It was, but it'd still make you wonder all the same. We waited too long to do things like this as a family. We won't be making that mistake again.

#######

I managed to catch the Kilkenny-Cork game last Sunday. There didn't seem to be any Irish bars showing it within a reasonable distance of where we were so I sent out a distress signal on Twitter. Sure enough, a chap from GAAGO got in touch and sent me a link. A few of us crowded around John's son Stephen's laptop and watched it. Cork were widely tipped to win and for that reason more than any other, I had a sneaking fancy for Kilkenny.

Cork have some superb hurlers, and Patrick Horgan underlined yet again how he's an absolute class act, but there's a flakiness to them which manifested again. They're missing a certain type of player. You look at the last team they had that was winning All-Irelands. Lovely hurlers on that too but you also had someone like Niall McCarthy at centre-forward, exactly what they're missing right now. They lack players that would spook you. When we beat them in 2006 it looked like it might take them a while to regroup but no one would have thought they'd still be without an All-Ireland at this stage.

I was waiting for them to come back at Kilkenny in the second half but it never really materialised and it was comfortable enough in the end.

What was most remarkable is that Kilkenny won with TJ Reid being held from play and they had an impact off the bench, which hasn't been the case for some time now. Conor

Browne was finally given a start and really proved his worth; I was delighted for him.

It's a big boost for them getting back to a semi-final. They're arguably exceeding expectations as you could say that Galway and Clare are both better than them and yet they didn't even reach the knockout stages.

They'll be underdogs against Limerick but will they go out believing that they can win? Absolutely. That's the only chance they have. Brian Cody won't spend the next couple of weeks trying to convince them, his body language will be enough to tell them. Never did we go out thinking that we couldn't win a game over the years. There was a fear of losing that drove us, but never a fear of the opposition. It won't be any different this time, regardless of the quality of the team Kilkenny field.

We also watched the Tipperary-Laois quarter-final. Niall Rigney was in touch with me many months ago when Eddie Brennan was being lined up as Laois manager as he was on the selection committee. He's really done a remarkable job with them. If they can just get some traction in the Leinster Championship, I reckon they have the ability to kick on from there. Of course, after their stirring victory over Dublin, Eddie is being talked of as a potential successor to Brian one day, just as was the case with Henry Shefflin a few months ago.

He's been a breath of fresh air in terms of how he allowed the players to let their hair down after winning the Joe McDonagh Cup and beating Dublin. Some managers would have cracked the whip with a game the following weekend in mind but that would have been counterproductive. I reckon he'd be very different to Cody in his managerial style. He has his head screwed on and would command respect but yet he would be someone that players would see as being very approachable and he wouldn't carry the same fear factor.

Eddie's very personable, as has been evident in how accessible he and his players have been with the media. Very un-Cody-like! While I'd say that Henry would be more like Brian in that respect if he were to become Kilkenny manager, I'd imagine that Eddie would be more open but not quite as open as he has been with Laois, purely because there's a very different profile to either county. But Henry or Eddie wouldn't want to be hanging around waiting for Brian to move on!

#######

My birthday was just far enough from Christmas to ensure that, as a youngster, I'd get another raft of the same presents a few months later.

I invariably got hurling gear; shorts, socks, helmets or hurls that I'd have knocked enough lumps out of to allow me to have another one a few months later. Handily, a fresh Manchester United strip would often be released at that time of the year too ahead of the new Premier League season. I remember one year I got to camp out in the back garden with my friends and we jumped the wall, into James Stephens' Larchfield pitch and wandered around town at all hours of the morning before sneaking back unnoticed.

Like at Christmas time, my day would be divided between my parents and there was never any commotion. My mother used to do a split shift in Rinnucini's restaurant in Kilkenny so I'd walk down that far with her in the evening and meet my father after he had finished his day's work in St Francis Abbey Brewery. We'd often end up at a hurling match that evening.

For my 21st, my mother put on a barbecue for me at home and had a good few people over but I couldn't indulge in burgers and beers in high summer during my first year on the Kilkenny senior panel. Indeed, I had to leave the party early to go to county under-21 training.

The standout among my birthdays is my 16th, when I went and bought a moped. I had just left school the month before and had started working with Philly Houlihan on my cabinet making apprenticeship, so I used it for going to and from work. A dark blue Yamaha. I got a loan from the Credit Union and my parents gave me a bit of money towards it too. It cost a couple of grand but, in fairness, the tax and insurance was cheap and it didn't cost too much to fill.

I thought I was it. Just after leaving school, I had a job and then my newfound independence was bolstered by having my own mode of transport.

A couple of my friends had mopeds too and we'd meet up, spinning around on them. Showing off in front of young ones. Of course, I put one of them up on the back of it one day and managed to throw her off it.

I felt like I was Maverick from the Top Gun film. Now, at a distance of 19 years, I realise I was probably something closer to Lloyd Christmas from Dumb and Dumber.

#######

Saturday, July 27, 2019

Definitely time has to be up, it has to be over, it has to be! Puck it up in the air as far as you can…Yessss! Yessss! Come on the Cats!

I guess you could say I got a bit carried away during the closing moments of the Kilkenny-Limerick game while on commentary with Brendan Hennessy and Mickey Walsh for *KCLR*, roaring over them into my microphone. The blood had long since drained from my face by then.

I was totally engrossed, my level of engagement having shot up several notches from the Leinster final. I was emotionally drained after it, my hands were shaking and my heart was pounding. This game really got under my skin, to a degree which surprised me. Playing was certainly far easier! But what an absolutely extraordinary evening it was at Croke Park.

It's been a long week since getting home from holidays on Tuesday. All of us – even Anne – said we'd happily have stayed on for another two weeks, though I was certainly lifted – catapulted – from my slumber this evening. Going into the game I couldn't see Kilkenny winning but I warmed to the way they were going about it within minutes of the throw-in, to such an extent that I completely flipped: I then couldn't see them losing.

There was an edge to them that hadn't been apparent heretofore. I feared that Limerick would be too physically strong for them beforehand but it just goes to show how you can overcome deficits like that when you're up for a game and totally focused.

I found the Leinster final defeat frustrating along with a lot of what Kilkenny have served up in the last few years. I started to think that maybe I was being too harsh on them because I might have been expecting things that they just weren't capable of. As I said, it didn't feel like a Brian Cody team. Too many of them didn't look, play or carry themselves like Brian Cody players. Well, between the Cork game and particularly this one, they've evolved into a Brian Cody team fairly rapidly. It was reminiscent of the 2006 All-Ireland final against Cork in how they swarmed all over Limerick.

Being truthful, Limerick were a little bit off. Brian always told us, 'If you're off a fraction, you're gone', and so it proved for them tonight. They were unlucky though. From our side of the ground, we didn't know at the time that Darragh O'Donovan's sideline ball had clipped Cillian Buckley's hurl right at the death and we all just leapt to our feet when a wide was signalled. But, again, it underlines Brian's greatest strength as a manager in that you can see how difficult it is to put All-Irelands back-to-back, yet he was virtually always able to instill a hunger like that of paupers in us.

Tactically he got it spot on. They had to get into Limerick's faces and not let them out of defence easily to allow them to play handy ball into the forwards.

Limerick were under pressure all evening and it told in some of the deliveries inside, which gave the Kilkenny backs the best chance of contesting the ball with the Limerick forwards, who were shooting under pressure throughout. John Donnelly only lasted 45 minutes but what a shift he put in. He just emptied himself. Conor Browne has proven his worth. TJ didn't score from play but he was just outstanding.

Looking out at it, I was thinking of how I'd love to be out there in the thick of it but then reality bites: you're 35 now, Eoin, not 25.

In time, the result will find its own context but, for now, it has to be Brian Cody's single greatest victory as Kilkenny manager given the quality of the Limerick team and where Kilkenny were coming from after a couple of lean years.

As I drove home tonight I pondered the three weeks that the players have ahead of them, by far the most exciting time for a hurler with all the little bits and pieces that go with building up to an All-Ireland final. A time when all you want to do is just go training and be with the lads.

'Ye lucky bastards,' I muttered to myself.

12

AUGUST

'What I consistently come back to, though, is Niall Donohue. I don't think about him every day, or even every week, but I suppose he's a reference point of sorts'

An August evening in Thurles. As autumn moved in, the Semple Stadium floodlights had seen out our All-Ireland semi-final replay with Waterford. The place was hopping at the end of a brilliant match which we had won thanks to Eoin Murphy's mighty leap and catch over his own crossbar to deny Pauric Mahony an equalising point at the death.

I played the full game, five weeks to the day since I had broken down on the phone to Brian Cody. That was something to be proud of. Just a few weeks after I had seen no value in the life I was living and had wanted it to end, I felt alive walking off the field that night. Charged.

That we had won was great, but this went beyond the winning and losing of a hurling match. If we had lost I'd have been disappointed, of course, but not crestfallen like I might have been before. Victory or defeat couldn't encroach on the satisfaction I felt at getting back to where I felt I belonged.

I didn't start the drawn game. I had only come back training 10 days beforehand. The Wednesday before the game, I was leaving training when Brian asked me for a word.

'How are you feeling?'

'Grand, feeling a lot better now, thanks.'

'Look,' he said, 'you won't be starting Sunday.'

'To be honest,' I said, 'I knew that was coming. I'm grand with it and I'm totally behind the lads. I'll do anything I can to help.'

'Good. Stay focused now and keep yourself right.'

I had my buzz back in training. I wasn't firing on all cylinders but I wanted to be there and was making a meaningful contribution to the group, at long last. I wasn't being as hard on myself when something didn't come off. I came on 10 minutes into the second half at a time when we were under the cosh. I did reasonably well. Worked hard. Was on a bit of ball. Did enough to win back my starting place for the replay. I'd taken a nice shot in the shoulder from Austin Gleeson but I shook it off as the week went on and was good to go. I didn't hurl up a storm in Thurles but I did my bit.

Although there were just five weeks between my breakdown and playing a full championship match, it was a very gradual process. The biggest step was the first one, when I went to see Tadhg and admitted that I had a problem, and that brought plenty of relief. I went back to him again four days later. I was slowly feeling better. 'That's grand, keep taking the tablets and if you've any problems, just ring me,' he said. We kept in touch after that. Clearly the medication was working. I was off work but keeping myself active. I'd do the washing, say, and other bits and pieces around the house. The kids were off school for the summer so I was looking after them. I'd head into town in the car. I might go for a run in the evening.

After a couple of weeks, I was itching to get back training, which was quite the turnaround in itself given that I was dragging my hurl and gear bag to Nowlan Park before that. You'd get enough of being around the house as well. People might say that they'd love to be at home every day but there's only so much of that you can take. So I was looking forward to getting back to work too.

Tadhg gave me the green light to return to training, two and a half weeks after I first presented myself to him in his practice. I went back in with Kilkenny and there wasn't a word about why I was away. I just slotted in. It would happen from time to time over the years that someone would be missing from training for a couple of weeks. Players might talk about it but no one would really know why. It wouldn't be something that Brian would address and he certainly wouldn't tell any of us privately. So we'd just get on with it.

I got back on the field for the Waterford games and, thankfully, had another final to look forward to against Tipperary. Although I was in the team again and saw that as a fine personal achievement in the circumstances, I wasn't so complacent to think that I was fully recovered and that that was it. It's a constant process and if I lose sight of that fact, I'm in trouble.

I felt that I was in a place where I could perform and be an asset to the team come the final, though unfortunately it didn't work out for us that day. I wasn't especially good or bad and was taken off in the second half in what proved to be my last game for Kilkenny. It reminded me of the 2010 final in that we were hanging in for a lot of the game and were eventually blown away.

Although it was a disastrous outcome for the team, I had a sense of perspective afterwards that would have been unthinkable earlier in my career, similar to how I felt after the Waterford win. But this time we actually had lost. In the players' lounge after the game, I got chatting to Cillian Buckley's girlfriend, Niamh. Cillian was in bits at the result, so upset that he couldn't even talk to her.

'I know how he feels,' I told her, 'but, look, you're going to get them and he just has to get over it.'

I probably would have been the very same as Cillian earlier in my career, possibly even if we had lost the final the year before but, after the previous couple of months, breaking down in tears over a hurling match was the last thing I was going to do. Was I disappointed? Absolutely. Devastated even? Yes – but in the context of it being a game of hurling and that's the crucial distinction to make. You have ups and downs in sport, that's just the nature of it. But you can't let it affect your life to too great a degree.

I've had some losses with the club in the meantime that have been extremely disappointing and have made me rather emotional, but it soon finds its place in the scheme of things. There's nothing wrong with being disappointed with the outcome of a game that you were involved in, but being pissed off at an event or occurrence in your life is a very different thing to being outright depressed.

My mood had improved gradually from the day of the phone call with Brian but that couldn't continue indefinitely or you'd just end up being delirious. I realised after the All-Ireland final that I had reached a plateau, that I was at the level I wanted to be at with my mental health. It was a good place to be. The challenge is to stay there and, while I've had my moments, I've made a pretty decent fist of that.

########

Monday, August 5, 2019

It had been a few months since I had seen Kim, and we finally got down to Cork to catch up with her and her family today. We've been in regular contact but at times it feels like the planets need to align in order for us to meet. I work Monday to Friday and Khaled, Kim's husband, works on Saturdays.

On Sundays I tend to have club training or a match or the kids might have something on and there aren't enough hours left in the day to make it worth our while to go up and down to Cork after all that. They had been to Lebanon, where Khaled comes from, for a couple of weeks before we went to Spain, so the bank holiday provided a bit of wriggle room and down we went. We agreed that we wouldn't leave it as long the next time.

It says a lot for our relationship that it didn't seem like that long since we had seen each other once we landed at her house. We picked up seamlessly from where we were in

.here was certainly no awkwardness. We went out for
the kids mingled with each other and then back to
s place for a while before we headed for home. Prior to
going on holidays, Holly had her hair dyed but it had gone off
a little so Khaled opened up his salon and brought her in to
put a toner through it. He touched up Anne's hair as well. It
was really nice of him; he didn't have to do that. He's mad to
get up and see me play a match – before it's too late!

Having not seen each other in a few months, a backlog
of presents had built up. I missed Kim's birthday, Colleen's
First Communion and Aisling's birthday so I gave them all
something today. I threw her other two daughters, Shannon
and Leah, a few quid as well so I was quite popular as we were
leaving and got a hug and a kiss from each of them!

In all, Kim and I have met five times now in the past year
and perhaps we could push it up to 10 over the next year. All
told, it's been a really enriching experience. Reflecting on the
past 12 months, Kim coming into my life has definitely been
the best thing that has happened to me.

########

Sunday, August 11, 2019

'You won't forget her birthday anyway – 11-8-11!' the doctor
quipped, just after Anne had given birth.

Ellie, our youngest, turned eight today. We had a gathering
at home for her with various family members coming over.
She'll have a proper birthday party once she's back in school
next month with her friends; she's far more excited about

that, naturally enough. She got another Reborn Baby doll to go with the one she got at Christmas and some other bits and pieces. Anne baked a cake for today but had to ditch it and buy one instead after the icing didn't quite work out for her!

Ellie was late coming when she was born in 2011. We had just beaten Waterford in the All-Ireland semi-final and were back with our clubs for a week. I had left Anne in her mother's house before I went to training and told her, 'By the time I come back you better be gone to the hospital!' She didn't disappoint.

My father was manning the club shop while we trained. It's just a hatch and to get out on the field he would have had to go back through the clubhouse. I could hear him calling me and then I could see him pouring a bottle of water out on the ground. I didn't know what he was at. When we were finished then he let a roar at me, 'Anne's waters are after breaking!' That's what he had been trying to signify with the bottle.

It was an exciting time, becoming a father again while building up to an All-Ireland final but, once Anne and Ellie came home, the game was key.

Anne, in fairness to her, did all the night feeds and moved into the spare room with the cot. We had discussed all of this well in advance. Anne didn't particularly mind doing night feeds whereas I found them really difficult. The trade-off was that she would sleep on in the mornings and I'd take over then. Everyone was a winner because she knew I'd be like a bear if I hadn't had my sleep!

Ellie has always been something of a daddy's girl but even more so since I came home from Syria. She won't let me out of her sight and wants to go everywhere with me.

'I didn't like you when you were in the army because you used to go off and leave me,' she often says.

'I only went off once, Ellie, because I had to go,' I'd reason.

'Yeah, but I don't like you leaving me.'

So she's been quite clingy the last few years. If I'm going out to training or for a pint, she could hit me with, 'Where are you going? Can I come with you?' It can be a little intense at times but, of course, it won't last. In another few years, as she moves towards her teens, she'll be running away from me.

Because she has an older brother and sister she's more mature than her age would suggest in some respects. God knows what she'll grow up to be but she can flip between wanting to be a vet one day to a hairdresser the next. She's hugely competitive and it's all about winning when it comes to her camogie team. Even when we were on holidays a few weeks back, she was losing her mind when the crazy golf wasn't working out for her. I think I know where she takes that from!

########

This is my first experience of Kilkenny being in an All-Ireland final as an ex-player and the build-up has been somewhat surreal. The fact that the final is now in August is a little strange and I would prefer the tradition of September.

Nonetheless, my mind has wandered back to the routine that went with it when I was playing. I wonder are they getting measured for their suits today? When's the media day? Then you snap out of it and reality bites: none of that is relevant to me anymore.

External expertise wouldn't have been something that was leaned on heavily by Brian Cody, but there were exceptions. In 2009 Pádraig Harrington was fresh from winning his third Major and we all jumped on a bus and went up to his home club, Stackstown, for a talk as the championship approached.

It was a grand idea in theory but I don't think we got much out of it. People may have a perception of the Kilkenny team as being intense, and they're probably right, but we were in the ha'penny place compared to Pádraig. He was talking about the left side of the brain and the right side and almost dissecting the human anatomy for us. That outlook obviously worked for him given his success, but a more simplistic one suited us better.

We got that from Gerry McEntee, the former Meath footballer, year after year in the build-up to All-Ireland finals. I think Mick Dempsey was the link to Gerry given their mutual football background.

Brian would only entertain having somebody if he was confident that it wouldn't get into the public domain or the media, and it never did with Gerry anyway. I don't recall having anyone else talk to us over the years bar him and Harrington. We were largely successful so we didn't need to have people in the whole time. If we hadn't been getting to finals maybe we'd think differently about it. As I see it, the danger of having too many people in is that there may be mixed messages from one person to the next and then you're left wondering who's right and who's wrong.

Gerry would usually come down for the last match session ahead of the final so there's every chance he'll have been in with the players this weekend. He'd watch the game we'd play among ourselves and then he'd talk to us afterwards. 'I won't keep ye too long now...' he'd always begin.

Our culture rhymed with his. He'd tell us how much respect he had for us, how he admired how we went about our business on and off the field with no bullshit ever seeping out. I suppose the Meath team he played on would have had similar traits to us. Ruthless and unflinching. 'Go right to the line but don't cross it,' he'd tell us, while referencing his sending off in the 1988 All-Ireland final replay, a game which he felt he was too wound up for.

He was probably saying much the same thing year after year but he'd put a slightly different twist on it each time and I'd always walk out thinking, 'He's after taking it to a new level again'. There was always the same sign-off that lost nothing in the repetition, however. He'd use an analogy of drowning someone, saying, 'Put your foot on his head and don't take it off until you see the last bubble...'

We'd often have a five-week build-up to All-Ireland finals and Gerry's address as the game approached was usually the trigger to start zoning in on what was ahead of us. You couldn't do that for five solid weeks or you'd be mentally drained by the time the game comes around. After his talks, my focus would be sharpened and over the course of the week I'd tap into it more and more, building myself up to the big day.

Do I miss not being involved at the moment? Yes, I do. It would have been much more difficult had they got to the final in 2017 but I'm three years away from it now. Also, whatever pangs I may feel now are comfortably offset by what goes with being an inter-county player for the rest of the year. The training, weekends away, not being able to go on a summer holiday, a curtailed social life. Things I was happy to forego when I was a younger man but not now. One of my best friends, Mark Wall, is getting married two days before the All-Ireland final. I'll miss a session with the club because of it and there's no problem. But you can't go to Brian Cody and say, 'I won't be at training this weekend, I have a wedding.'

One thing that's common to finals whether you're a current or ex-player, however, is hassle with tickets. Obviously it's a lot less feverish for me now than when I was playing but I still have a lot of people to sort out. I texted Jimmy Walsh, the county board chairman, asking for 12 tickets. 'I'll do what I can but definitely not 12!' he replied. When I was playing, I might process more than 100 tickets. We'd get about 10 complimentary and then I'd have requests coming in from all angles on top of that.

'Are you getting tickets for the whole barracks or what?' Cody said to me one year, a couple of weeks out from a final.

'No, just around the club and a couple of friends and that.'

'Get them sorted now this week, I don't want to hear about them next week.'

I tried to have them out of my hair come the week of the game. On reflection, I probably should have handed them over to a family member to sort out, as many players do. You learn as you go.

In the early days I'd get tickets for certain people only to be told, 'Oh I'm alright, I don't need them now.' So I demanded money up front thereafter. Others might say, 'Jesus, they're shit tickets!' when you handed them over. They were placed at the bottom of the list come the following year.

I don't need a ticket myself as I'm on duty with *KCLR* once again. I'm glad that I'm involved in the game in some capacity that way. I'll find it easier than being out in the middle of the stand, I reckon.

########

When I look back on my career with Kilkenny, the games we had with Tipperary are the most special. By a huge distance. Thankfully we won a lot more of them than we lost but they were brilliant games to be involved in. You knew what you were going to get and that you had to be at your very best. Otherwise, you weren't going to win. Even in 2009, when a lot of us hadn't faced them in a championship match before, we were convinced of that much. We had to be at our best. If we weren't, given what Tipperary threw at us in that All-Ireland final, we'd have been blown away.

That ties in with Brian Cody's single greatest strength as a manager – his ability to banish complacency. I'd imagine anyone that's played under him would agree. He's brilliant at keeping lads motivated and then driving new players to reach the same levels. That's why he's still in the job after all these years. I'd say that in all my time with Kilkenny, the only big game where we were guilty of complacency was the 2012 Leinster final against Galway and we were 14 points down at half-time. When you think of it like that, it's an incredible feat of management.

Our modern rivalry with Tipperary started with Liam Sheedy's appointment. They hadn't really been mapped for years before that. They beat us in a league semi-final in Nowlan Park in 2008, Sheedy's first season. I was just back from a tour of duty in Kosovo so I wasn't playing. They went on to win the league and the Munster title and though they lost the All-Ireland semi-final to Waterford, it was clear that they were coming.

When they came to Nowlan Park in the league in 2009, the defeat the year before would have been referenced by Brian, that they weren't going to dictate to us in our own ground this time. We filleted them, 5-17 to 1-12. They recovered to reach the league final against us a few weeks later and we knew they weren't going to lie down again. I suppose that's the day that the rivalry really started to take off. They threw absolutely everything at us in a fierce contest, but we eventually burned them off after extra time.

Eddie Brennan later said that the league medal he won that day was one of his most treasured possessions from his career. I wouldn't go so far as to put it over any of the All-Irelands, but it was certainly very satisfying. We weren't handed anything, we had to work extremely hard for every score. The games were played at a crazy pace. You'd barely have a chance to catch your breath and the ball was down on top of you again. Then it's gone and back on top of you once more. There were any amount of breathless regulation league games too which nearly became as important because you didn't want to show any weakness.

When we played them in the 2009 All-Ireland final, it had a different feel to the previous couple of years when we'd beaten Limerick and Waterford.

The whole thing was ramped up. Tradition matters. The two counties hadn't met an awful lot in the championship over the previous 40 years but Kilkenny people have long memories and for decades, up to 1967, Kilkenny just couldn't beat Tipp. That's not something that we'd get hung up about inside the camp but you could still sense it from people around the county. This was different.

My cousins in Callan would say to me, 'Don't let them Tipp c**ts win, they'll be over the border on Sunday night, they'll be down in the pubs in Callan rubbing it in. I wouldn't be going up to Mullinahone to drink if Kilkenny won but they somehow think they have the right to come down here.'

The 2009 All-Ireland final was probably the best of all the games we played. We rode our luck that day. The penalty we won was fortunate but Richie Power was definitely fouled, though the original offence was outside the penalty area so a free in was probably the right call. I think Henry would have gone for goal either way. We were struggling at the time and I don't think a point would have given us the lift we needed.

I know I was infused with fresh energy when he scored. I won a ball straight away and gave it to Martin Comerford for another goal and then I clipped a couple of points. Even the way Pádraic Maher and Paul Curran collided going for the ball before I set up Martin was an indication of how Tipp became flustered after going behind. The game had gone a bit helter-skelter at that stage after Benny Dunne's red card and we closed it out well. They hurled better than we did on the day but struggled to put us away.

When push came to shove, that little bit of doubt must have been in their minds. They missed goal chances. They weren't clinical. If it was the other way round and we outhurled them to that degree, we probably would have won rather comfortably, as we sometimes did subsequently.

We had an ability to stay in games when we weren't playing particularly well. It came down to hard work. If things weren't flowing for you, go and get a tackle in or a hook or a block. That gives everyone else a lift. If you're corner-forward and not in the game, you took it upon yourself to change that. 'Just come out for five minutes, do something, get a tackle in and go back in if you want,' Brian would say. The work comes before the hurling.

We respected the Tipperary players as hurlers and on All Star trips we tended to mix fairly well. I had good time for Paddy Stapleton and I got on well with Conor O'Brien having been on a stag with him once. Eoin Kelly was a grand fella off the field and Brendan Maher too.

But a lot of the shit that went with Tipp rubbed us up the wrong way. This nonsense of pointing to their heads after a score, for example. It was nearly as if they were trying to convince themselves that they could beat us. When they did beat us in 2010, there was a *Sunday Game* ad on TV for a year or two afterwards where Noel McGrath was coming out to Kelly, pointing to his head. I'd roll my eyes every time I saw it.

The 2010 defeat was incredibly difficult to take. The worst loss of my career. We lost more than an All-Ireland final that day. Realistically, while we won plenty after it, that group of players wasn't going to get back to a stage where we could win five-in-a-row. The hype was different that year to what we'd experienced when going for three-in-a-row and four-in-a-row. The wheels just came off after the semi-final against Cork. Henry did his cruciate in the game and then Brian Hogan broke his finger in training. If we had the two of those fully fit, there's no doubt in my mind that we would have won.

Brian was never going to be right to play but Henry put in a phenomenal effort and was back training a couple of weeks beforehand. That brought a carnival with it, and thousands flocked to some of our sessions. It didn't bother me at the time but, looking back on it, it was hardly ideal preparation and Brian took the decision on the back of that to shut the gates of Nowlan Park in subsequent years. It's something that's happened in Kerry in recent years too and it makes absolute sense in this day and age. With all the analysis that goes on, why would you leave yourself open to such scrutiny, not to mention the distraction?

The first night that Henry came back training, you could tell that he was minding himself a bit but, after that, he was back to himself from what I could see. It was demoralising when he went off so early in the final, though you're just trying to get on with the game. But he was a massive loss. Canice Hickey, who was on the panel at the time, later told me, 'I knew we were beat at half-time because all our heads were down.' We were still in touch at that stage but we were struggling. Tipp were on top. Henry was gone off. We were without our centre-back and John Tennyson was playing there instead with his own knee patched up. As big as Henry's absence was, I always felt that the loss of Hogie was even greater.

Even the first goal that Tipp got, Lar Corbett holding off Noel Hickey to make the catch. The fact that the two of them were so isolated in that part of the field told you the game was being played on Tipp's terms. And, let's face it, when a high ball comes in between those two, you're only expecting one winner and it's not Corbett. They got a huge lift from that goal and we were always chasing it. When they got the second and third goals, we were goosed as far as I was concerned.

The banquet and the homecoming was an incredible drag. I'd never experienced that side of it before. You're getting introduced to the crowd and you're embarrassed by it because you've lost.

On the field, Tipp could be nasty enough. Declan Fanning and I had many's the battle. He'd always be mouthing and pulling and dragging out of you. Sometimes you'd give him a dig back and other times you'd ignore him. The best thing to do is just put the ball over the bar but at times he did get under my skin, I have to admit. Now, we didn't exactly field 15 altar boys ourselves but I don't believe we stooped to their level. Pádraic Maher's pull on Michael Rice in the 2012 semi-final was referenced in our camp for a long time afterwards. 'Show them no respect, look what they did.' It was reckless. Michael wasn't right for a long time.

I was always especially nervous coming into the Tipp games because I knew they could beat us. You'd be terrified of losing. The 2013 qualifier game in Nowlan Park is probably the one that stands out the most.

The atmosphere was phenomenal. I didn't go outside the door the week of that match, only for work. Even in work I didn't go to the canteen. The consequences of losing the game would run through your mind. Losing would have tarnished everything we had done. The four-in-a-row would certainly have lost its sheen.

It's a game that we really shouldn't have won given how we were struggling at the time but we just couldn't countenance being put out of the championship on our own pitch by

Tipperary. Whatever had to happen, that just could not happen. That was reinforced all week by Brian and the players. Of course, you can't just decide to win a game and it automatically happens but there was a level of defiance about us that evening which meant that Tipp would have had to produce something absolutely extraordinary to beat us. I knew that much as soon as I landed in the dressing room that evening.

We were running on empty and Henry and Michael Fennelly, who had been injured, were fast-tracked back onto the bench for that game, something Brian wouldn't ordinarily do. We were out on the pitch warming up when their names were announced. The place went bananas. The ground was virtually full already. We'd beaten Tipp in the league final at Nowlan Park a couple of months earlier but this was something else.

It was cruel hot, too. I played plenty of times in a full Croke Park with almost four times the crowd but it was nothing like this. In Croke Park, the crowd is that bit further away from you and at an All-Ireland final a lot of the crowd is neutral. But it was pure tribal that night.

Why did beat we them far more often than they beat us? Was it because we just had much better hurlers? I don't think so, really. It was much of a muchness in that respect. I believe it came down to our mental strength. We were able to back it up time after time; they weren't. They were sloppy off the field. You'd hear rumours of their players acting the bollocks, wrecking places and fighting. Getting notions about themselves. Stuff that didn't happen with us, at least certainly not on that scale. That matters.

Then, of course, there was the Lar Corbett debacle in the

2012 semi-final, when he went out to mark Tommy Walsh. Who sends out a forward to mark a back? Like, even if that was the instruction from the management, wouldn't you think after two minutes that he'd conclude, 'Fuck it, I'm not doing this, running around after him like an eejit'. Where was their mental strength then? Brian trusted us to do the right thing on the field. If we saw a switch that needed to be made, it was done. 'Don't wait for me to tell ye,' he'd say.

Corbett later said that that episode with Tommy was born out of how Jackie had tied him up the year before and that he felt he wasn't going to be let play. But surely your attitude should be, 'This lad got the better of me last year, I'm going to show him this time' rather than just accepting defeat before the ball was even thrown in? I'd rather have another crack at him and go down swinging.

We lost a lot of respect for Tipperary after 2012. I think they know that they let themselves down badly. What the fuck were they at? I must say, I enjoyed sewing it into them that day. We beat them by 18 points and they just let us do it. You could see them wilt in a way that they hadn't before.

They beat us in the 2010 and 2016 All-Ireland finals. In 2010, we were missing Hogie and Henry after a few minutes. In 2016, we were a shadow of what we had been. But when both teams were at their best, we always beat them. We were on our knees in 2013 and they couldn't take us. It was sheer grit that got us there, probably the one area they couldn't match us in.

The 2016 final defeat wasn't as difficult to take as 2010, even though it proved to be my last game for Kilkenny and it obviously wasn't the way you'd want to sign out. We had run out of road and, personnel-wise, it was the weakest Kilkenny panel that I'd been a part of. Brian used subs sparingly over the previous few years and the fact that we were in a position to win three-in-a-row going into that final was one of his greatest feats.

There was so much space in front of our full-back line that day and Séamus Callanan filled his boots. Brian was criticised for not making a change and Jackie was obviously disappointed that he wasn't sent in to try and stem the tide. He probably should have made a change, to be fair, given how much trouble we were in.

But, in truth, that was the day when we were found out. We were an ordinary side by the standards of what had gone before and even the Tipp team that beat us wasn't as good as what we had faced six or seven years earlier. That was the best team that I played against.

On the whole, I would say that we were always utterly convinced that we were going to beat Tipperary. We wouldn't have to check ourselves with 10 minutes to go. We just kept going about what we were doing until the final whistle blew. Maybe they had a sense of, 'We have them at this stage, what do we do? Will we kick on or won't we?'

If you drilled down far enough, not only did we expect we were going to win, but I suspect they probably did too.

########

It's a new era for the Kilkenny-Tipperary rivalry now, as I see it. Certainly for Kilkenny anyway. Richie Hogan will be the only one from the Kilkenny team that started the 2009 final, though Tipperary have a few more survivors so maybe they'd see it as the same old Kilkenny – and that could be their downfall. Tipp were comfortably beaten by Kilkenny in last year's league final when they really should have been winning that game. Again, in this year's league, Kilkenny beat them by a point in Thurles when Tipp had a far stronger team on paper. They'll have a stronger team on paper in the All-Ireland final too but hurling isn't played on paper.

If Kilkenny reach the same levels as they did against Limerick, I couldn't see them losing. Make it a battle, not a shootout. I'm sure that the Tipperary players will say and honestly believe, at this remove, that Kilkenny have nothing over them psychologically but the truth of that only reveals itself when it's all on the line with a few minutes to go. You can never be sure what the subconscious has stored.

Tipperary could win this final well but if Kilkenny are within touching distance come the last 10 minutes, I feel they'll do it.

########

Sunday, August 18, 2019

About 15 minutes before the All-Ireland final got underway today, my arms were shaking and my legs started rattling. The pre-match nerves had gone into overdrive.

I just wanted the game to get underway so that I could relax and tune into that rather than being so pent up with anticipation. It was a weird type of nervousness that I'd never experienced before. Almost like an out of body experience.

Kilkenny were in an All-Ireland final and here I was observing the whole thing.

Of course, I'd done that before as a young lad but now I know exactly what the whole day entails as a player. And here I was in the press box, looking down at the lads going through their warm-up and visualising myself being a part of it, as I was so many times before. Puffing hard, trying to get my second wind. Taking a swig of the water bottle. Even when the parade was taking place, I was breathing to the same rhythm as I had when I was a player stepping around Croke Park behind the band. In through the nose, out through the mouth. Just looking at the head in front of me, blanking out all the colour and noise. Getting myself ready for what was coming.

I sang the anthem, like I always did at Croke Park, and at that stage my heart was nearly jumping out of my chest. It was like all the blood had rushed to my head. My hands were sweating. I just wanted the game to start. I had been wound up at times for the previous couple of games I had been at, but nothing like this.

My nerves were heightened by the fact that there was now something for them to lose. I didn't expect them to beat Limerick so I was relaxed before that game but today I really felt they could win. I was worried for them that they wouldn't produce and be blown out of the water. The build-up to the game took off locally from the middle of the week and the tension had started to build in me on Friday morning, though Mark's wedding proved to be a distraction from it. The butterflies began to flutter in my stomach again during the drive to Dublin yesterday though. I was appearing on *Up*

For The Match, a show I had often watched on final eve to pass the time.

It was good craic, all told, primarily due to Joe Hayes, the former Tipperary hurler. I was appearing with Paddy Stapleton and Tipperary dual player Orla O'Dwyer but Joe regaled us before and afterwards in the green room. He was going on with Fan Larkin but they didn't restrict their needling to when the cameras were rolling and there was good banter between them too. I'd never met Joe before but he'd have you in stitches.

I was chatting to Lar Corbett for a bit too. The two of us had taken part in the *GAA Hour* podcast a couple of nights earlier as well. I would have spoken to him very little over the years, just once or twice on All Star trips, and he came across as a nice chap, as did the other Tipp lads. I'm sure as the years roll on and a bit of distance from our playing days is established, we'll be able to look back and have a good laugh at instances from our careers that we'd have been very uptight over at the time.

That was reflected in what Paddy spoke about when we were on air together. There's a huge rivalry between the counties but that fell by the wayside once word went out last year for the benefit match for his late sister, Amanda. Everybody that could be there put their hand up.

I wasn't on live commentary duty today. Along with Adrian Ronan, I was just providing analysis before and after the game as well as at half-time. Once the game started and Kilkenny were doing well, my nerves subsided. The start of the game was remarkably similar to the semi-final but with one marked difference: Kilkenny didn't capitalise on their dominance with a goal this time. Had they got one, it would have been worth more than three points in the circumstances. They had one great chance through Colin Fennelly though John McGrath did brilliantly to hook him and Kilkenny looked dangerous every time they attacked.

Tipp were always going to have their period but I wasn't too worried when they reeled off 1-3 to go a point in front. Kilkenny had been hurling well and I was confident that they would come again. And then, coming up to half-time, Richie Hogan caught Cathal Barrett as he attempted to shoulder him out over the line. I didn't think it was a red card in real time and I saw nothing to change my mind from the first couple of replays on the monitor in front of us. But once I watched the final angle, where you could see Richie catching him flush on the chin, I said to Adrian beside me, 'He could send him off for this'. And that's exactly what James Owens did.

By the letter of the law, was it a red card? Yes. There have been others for similar offences this year, but then there have been more that have gone unpunished. That's the frustrating thing. Richie was upended himself against Cork by Bill Cooper when Owens was also in charge but only flashed a yellow card, while Cillian Buckley was lucky not to walk against Limerick for a challenge on Barry Nash. Same with Ronan Maher on Peter Casey in the Munster final.

And yet, while we want consistency, do I really want all of those to be red cards? No, I don't. The game is so fast now that you're going to have mistimed challenges with no malice attached. I think it should be recognised for what it is and cut the players some slack. The dirt – the real dirt – is gone out of hurling these days.

Tipperary's semi-final win over Wexford, when they came back to win with 14 men, was very much an exception and probably down to Wexford's inexperience more than anything else, but generally once a team suffers a red card at a critical juncture these days, they're going to lose. Players are so fit nowadays and management teams so tactically aware that you won't get away with it and Kilkenny just couldn't cope.

There was an inevitability about the outcome which was underscored by Tipp's two early second half goals. It was a long way to the final whistle at that stage and my arms and legs had long since stopped jigging.

I would accept that Tipperary looked the more likely victors at the time of the red card but you just don't know how the game would have panned out with 15 on 15. John O'Dwyer barely hit a ball in the first half but then he was running into space and popping it over from the sideline. Would that have been happening if the game was more compact with the full complement on both sides? It's all conjecture now.

But Tipperary are certainly worthy champions. They came back from a serious beating in the Munster final that I thought would finish them and they've ended the decade with three All-Irelands, which is a fair achievement for Brendan Maher, Pádraic Maher, Séamus Callanan and Noel McGrath along with the injured Patrick 'Bonner' Maher. They're fantastic hurlers. Callanan has been lethal for the past few years now. McGrath has bounced back from having cancer. Brendan Maher has recovered from a cruciate injury and I'm sure Bonner will too. You have to hand it to them.

I'm disappointed for the Kilkenny players but it's certainly not all doom and gloom. I don't believe the way the game finished out will be too demoralising for them in the long-term. In fact, I think it will spur them on next year and beyond. There was no great structure to the team until recently but suddenly Cody has built a solid foundation and they'll go on from here, I'm sure. For a couple of years there, I was a somewhat indifferent former player but they drew out the Kilkenny supporter in me this year and I'm grateful to them for that.

I couldn't see where the next All-Ireland was coming from not so long ago. Now I can.

########

If depression was once some sort of vague term that washed over me as I went about my daily life, it certainly isn't now. Things like, say, the Celtic striker Leigh Griffiths taking time away from the game to look after his mental health would make you stop and think.

I wouldn't claim that I know what he's going through because everyone's situation is unique but I'd imagine he had a somewhat similar experience where it was difficult for him to admit that he had a problem initially. It's a very hard thing to do, publicly or privately. I would have been fearful of walking around Kilkenny that people would be looking at me and saying, 'That lad's depressed'. That's why I went to a counsellor in Waterford rather than someone locally-based in the months after my breakdown. Now? That wouldn't bother me at all.

What I consistently come back to, though, is Niall Donohue. I don't think about him every day, or even every week, but

I suppose he's a reference point of sorts. When we marked each other those few times in 2012, one thing that struck me about him was his fierce determination. Another was that he always appeared to be wrecked, just out on his feet. He could be the same in the first minute of a game as he was in the last. But then he'd get the ball and tear down the wing, jet-heeled, very skilful with a lovely strike.

I remember Tommy Walsh ringing me in October 2013 to tell me that Niall had died. The two of us went up to the wake in Kilbeacanty along with Michael Rice. I can vividly recall the devastation of his family and thinking that this was absolutely horrendous. And when I was at my lowest and considering suicide, it's scenes like that that would help snap me out of it. Not indefinitely, mind, because those thoughts would still come back at a later stage and last for longer and become increasingly appealing, but perhaps it helped to keep the wolf from the door long enough so that I could finally get the help that I desperately needed.

There's a bit of a paradox there too in that I think of him more now, when I'm well, than I did when I was ill. I might see something on Twitter or hear something on the radio that takes me back to that wake and the drive up to his house and the crowds converging on it, cars parked in a field. I don't think of it in terms of it could have been me, but more scolding myself for not recognising my own predicament and saying something a lot sooner.

There's a much better balance to my lifestyle now. Certainly my relationship with alcohol is a lot healthier. It wasn't that I had a drink problem or was headed towards alcoholism or anything remotely like that, but I haven't drank shorts since

2016. That's made a massive difference as I don't invite misery on myself with the horrendous hangovers that they used to bring. Now I just drink a few pints and I enjoy them, but I know where to draw the line. I might be somewhat hungover and tired the next day but I can function. I'm not lying in bed, pulling the covers over my head.

Have I banished suicidal thoughts completely since 2016? No, they've returned a few times since, even in spite of everything. It's invariably linked to my medication. I went to the counsellor in Waterford for a couple of months at the outset and then it got to a point where I didn't need to anymore; it had run its course. I need to keep in touch with the doctor every now and again. I'm not terribly well organised by nature so when my medication runs out I sometimes go without it for a few days and that's all it would take. I could slip into a daydream and have those negative thoughts again. Back to snapping at Anne at home, but she can see the triggers and watches out for me.

'Did you take your tablet today?' she'd ask.

'No, I haven't got them, I have to get a new prescription.'

'Well go and get them because you're like an anti-Christ!'

That's why, at this stage of my life at least, it's an ongoing condition that has to be managed and the vast majority of the time I do that quite well by simply taking my medication. I don't know if I'll be required to take that 20mg Lexapro tablet for the rest of my life or whether I'll be weaned off it at some stage but it's assessed on an ongoing basis. And it's not just stopping taking them for a few days that will drag my mood down either. I have to make sure I have the right balance in my life, something I didn't have when I was working in Pfizer.

The hours that went with the shift work and the commute to Saggart on top of it gradually brought me down and it came to a head after just over a year of working there. I was jumpy and couldn't relax. I seemed to be wrecked the whole time and unable to sleep.

My dose was increased and I was instructed to take a month off work by the doctor. But he told me that, once I went back on the shifts, it would eventually get on top of me again so that's when I knew I had to look for something else. Pfizer were understanding and my supervisor was very compassionate.

There was nothing wrong with the job, it just didn't suit me and when I moved on to Transfermate, the right balance in my working life was restored and that's been maintained with *KCLR*. As I've said, there's no room for complacency but the crucial difference now is that I'm aware of my problem so that gives me the ability to manage it. For years I was blind to it, so it naturally got worse.

I haven't told many people about my episodes of depression. My family were aware of it, but perhaps not the full extent, and then virtually nobody outside of that apart from the medical professionals and Brian Cody.

I'm not ashamed of it but, as I've said, it's not my style to draw it up in conversation or post on social media about it. That might work for some people, and good luck to them, but it's not for me.

While I don't have a problem with it being out there now as a result of this book, I'm not sure how comfortable I would be talking to people outside of my circle about it face to face. Now, maybe I'd be grand, but I don't really know because it's never happened. There was one instance where I did discuss it with someone for a very particular reason, however.

Mikey Drennan was an outstanding underage hurler in our club but he's a really talented soccer player too. Good enough to be snapped up by Aston Villa as a teenager. He had his issues with depression, which he has spoken publicly about, and after he ended up back in the League of Ireland playing with Shamrock Rovers, he took a break from the game as a result of his problems. He resumed playing hurling with us but it was felt that maybe he wasn't really giving it his all. Mikey would certainly have played senior hurling for Kilkenny if he hadn't gone to England and I knew he could bring a lot to our team.

So I asked him to meet me for a coffee one day. We spoke about how he was and what he had been through and a lot of what he said rhymed with my experience.

'I know what you're going through at the moment,' I told him. 'I suffered with it myself. But it does get better.'

At the end of the conversation he said, 'I'm delighted to be home and I'm going to give hurling a good lash.'

He was true to his word and really bought into it for the rest of that campaign in 2017. He was on the team as we got to the county final but unfortunately we were well beaten by Dicksboro. He's since gone back playing soccer with Sligo Rovers and now he's with St Patrick's Athletic. I'm delighted for him and hope that his career continues to progress.

There's almost something glib about how people say 'just talk about it' when it comes to depression. There's more to it than that. At least there was for me. Until I got that phone call from Brian Cody, I had no idea that there was anything wrong with me. So how could I have talked about it? If it was another few weeks or months down the line, I could have taken my own life without even realising that I had depression. That's how bad it was.

Others will join the dots and grasp that they have it, but people in my situation wouldn't get why they have to talk because they just don't understand that something is wrong.

Ultimately, it's down to the individual to conclude that they have a problem. They need those around them to see it too and take the appropriate steps. Simply having a chat won't fix it. Bring them to the doctor. The doctor then needs to ask the right questions. It requires the person then to be as honest as they can possibly be, and that's not easy.

Anne did all of these things with me initially and just because I didn't buy into it at the time doesn't mean that it was the wrong thing for her to have done. Second time around in 2016, it worked, thankfully.

My experiences with depression have taught me a hell of a lot. I've learned what it is for starters, or at least what it is for me. I've learned how it can take your thoughts to extremely dark places.

I've learned that it can happen to anyone, when once I thought of it as some vague affliction that affected faceless individuals.

Depression doesn't discriminate and there's no good reason why I should have it and someone else shouldn't. Look at all I had in my life when it was at its worst: a great family, a hurling career I could only have dreamed of with the most successful team in the history of the game.

None of that shielded me from it.

Now, I'm watching All-Ireland finals instead of winning them. And yet, though I'm fully aware that the future brings no guarantees, I'm truly happy and my life is more complete now than it ever was.

A life without camouflage.

THANKS

I would like to say a huge and very sincere thank you to everyone that played a part in my career and, more importantly, my life. Obviously my family are to the fore-front of that. To my father, Allen, I would never have had the career I had without you ferrying me around for a match or training. You always had confidence that I could be the best. To my mother, Lucy, it really didn't matter what happened on the pitch, all you wanted was for me to be happy and ok. I can never repay the support you have given me.

My dad's wife Veronica and my mother's husband Paddy have been nothing but supportive in every way too, along with my sisters Louise and Kim and my brothers Anthony and Allen. Since coming into my life, Kim has brought something to be incredibly excited about and thankful for. I now have a brother-in-law, Khaled, and four beautiful nieces, Shannon, Colleen, Aisling and Leah.

To my wife, Anne, who has been ever-present since I started my journey with Kilkenny. You have been there, not just for me, but for our children, Mark, Holly and Ellie throughout and kept the show on the road. I will never be able to repay you or the children for your patience and understanding but I will continue to try.

Brian Cody deserves a huge thank you, ranging from my time in St Patrick's De La Salle to the great days in Croke Park. He always believed in me when others had questions. To all of Brian's backroom teams, from selectors to medical staff, I will be eternally grateful. Special mention to Dr Tadhg Crowley for his professionalism at all times.

I would also like to thank all of the officers of Kilkenny GAA County Board and the supporters club, as well as all the teachers in St Patrick's De La Salle and St Kieran's College for everything they have done for me.

Most of all, I want to thank James Stephens GAA Club for making me what I am today as a person and as a hurler. They nurtured my talent from a very young age along with showing me how to behave both on and off the field. Great men like Michael 'Sla' Slattery and Seán Brennan are two that spring to mind but there were many more exceptional people in the club who helped me along the way over the years. The Village is always in my heart and I am proud and honoured to be part of such a brilliant and historic club.

Sadly, as the production of this book entered its closing stages, news of Brother Damien Brennan's passing emerged. Brother Damien touched many lives and was a great friend and confidante to several Kilkenny hurlers, myself included. He will be sorely missed.

I would like to thank the Department of Defence and all of its members, especially those who I served with in the Third infantry battalion in Kilkenny and overseas.

Sincere thanks to Pat Nolan for all his hard work and

professionalism at all times. He was a joy to deal with and to be around. Thanks also to Damian Lawlor for putting us in touch.

To Paul Dove and Reach Sport for all their hard work and professionalism, thank you. They have been nothing short of brilliant since first contact was made. Thanks also to Simon Hess and all at Gill Hess.

Hurling was always what I wanted to do. To represent The Village at all grades and then to play for and captain Kilkenny, I have achieved everything that I ever wanted and hoped for.

To the Kilkenny players that I was blessed to share a dressing room with: we took our hurling deadly serious but we always had a truly magnificent time off the field too. From the training weekends to the celebrations, and sometimes the commiserations.

We always made the best of the time we had together, forging memories that will last a lifetime.

Eoin Larkin,
September 2019

I wish to start by thanking Eoin Larkin for entrusting me to write his story. He was a hurler I always admired on a team that, at their best, I found mesmerising to watch. It was very gratifying to gain a deeper insight into some of their internal workings while putting this book together.

Eoin had an all-or-nothing approach to his hurling which, to his credit, he also applied to this book. Nothing was off the table. That's gold dust to a ghostwriter. Readers can see straight through autobiographies where the subject is being cagey and Eoin was determined not to add to that particular catalogue of books. He was a pleasure to work with over the past year and exudes the humility that was a trademark of the Kilkenny team he played on.

Thanks to Eoin's wife Anne along with Mark, Holly and Ellie for their hospitality as I spent long hours in their living room asking endless questions of him.

Special thanks must go to Damian Lawlor, who directed Eoin towards me once he decided to commit his story to print. Damian was also a very helpful sounding board over the course of the past 12 months or so.

Eoin is not the first, and may not be the last, personality from the great Kilkenny hurling team on which he played to write a book. With that in mind, I felt there was a need to do something different in how we went about putting it together. To that end, Professor Paul Rouse, a fellow Tullamore man who I've known since my youth, was a huge help. The idea was to present Eoin's life as it is in the present and use it to reflect on his past and project what the future may hold, insofar as that was possible.

Like Damian and Paul, Paul Keane is an outstanding author and a great friend who provided me with invaluable feedback as I worked my way through the book. I can't thank him enough for this. A word of thanks as well to Enda McEvoy and my *Irish Daily Mirror* colleague Michael Scully.

Thanks also to Vincent Hogan for endorsing the book. Coming from someone of his standing, it was very humbling.

I have worked for Reach PLC (formerly Trinity Mirror) since 2007. It is a company of many, many strands and I only came to realise in recent years, after it moved into the Irish market, that it is also a publisher of sports books. Reach Sport has been a pleasure to deal with as we brought this project to a conclusion and I'd especially like to thank Executive Editor Paul Dove for his professionalism throughout. Credit should also go to Senior Executive Art Editor Rick Cooke and Senior Designer Lee Ashun for their design vision. Thanks also to Simon Hess, Declan Heeney and all at Gill Hess for their promotional work.

To conclude, I wish to acknowledge everyone in Tullamore GAA Club and, last though certainly not least, special thanks to my family for their unflinching support and interest in my endeavours.

Pat Nolan,
September 2019